First edition copyright © 2021 by Melody Tyden

This edition copyright © 2024 by Melody Tyden

All rights reserved.

The characters and events portrayed in this book are fictitious. Any similarity to real persons, living or dead, is coincidental and not intended by the author.

No part of this book may be reproduced, or stored in a retrieval system, or transmitted in any form or by any means, electronic, mechanical, photocopying, recording, or otherwise, without express written permission of the publisher.

Cover design by: Aisling Elizabeth

It Figures

MELODY TYDEN

Thank you to Kemely Parfrey for all your help in editing this story, and for loving Amy and Austin just as much as I do!

Contents

Playlist	1
1. Chapter One	3
2. Chapter Two	15
3. Chapter Three	35
4. Chapter Four	51
5. Chapter Five	65
6. Chapter Six	81
7. Chapter Seven	93
8. Chapter Eight	111
9. Chapter Nine	121
10. Chapter Ten	141
11. Chapter Eleven	155
12. Chapter Twelve	169
13. Chapter Thirteen	187
14. Chapter Fourteen	205
15. Chapter Fifteen	215

16. Chapter Sixteen	227
The Story Continues	235
Keep In Touch	237

Playlist (Amy & Austin)

- **Still Hurting** - *The Last 5 Years* (Sherie Rene Scott)
- **The One That Got Away** - Katy Perry
- **Only Love Can Hurt Like This** - Paloma Faith
- **Photograph** - Ed Sheeran
- **Evergone** - Christina Perri
- **Goodbye Until Tomorrow** - *The Last 5 Years* (Sherie Rene Scott, Norbert Leo Butz)
- **Mirrors** - Justin Timberlake
- **Chasing Cars** - Snow Patrol

Chapter One

~Amelia~

I almost made it out the door that morning without hearing his name.

As I picked up the remote to turn off the small TV in my dorm room, I glanced up just in time to see the local news anchor smiling blandly into the camera.

"Speaking of the Olympics, ice dancers Grace Matthews and Austin Black will be unveiling their new program in a couple of weeks, the one they hope will take them…"

My chest tightened as I pressed down on the 'off' button, the screen going black before I heard anything else. In the dark screen, I could see myself reflected instead: my short, dark bob and my thick-rimmed glasses with my eyes wide behind them. Tossing the remote back down, my hand went to the four-leaf clover necklace I always wore, the familiar metal cool beneath my fingers.

"We make our own luck," I whispered to myself. "And today's going to be my day."

A couple of minutes later, a gust of cool air hit my face as I opened the main door of the dorm and stepped outside.

"Finally! I'm freezing my butt off out here!" My friend, Gaby, danced from foot to foot, shivering dramatically. Her curly black hair fought against the white toque she wore, trying to push it off her head while she tugged it back down.

I shot her a grin as we began walking briskly down the street. It *was* cold for late September, I'd give her that, but we both knew the *real* cold hadn't arrived yet. "It's only just below freezing. When I used to train..."

"Yeah, yeah, I know," she cut me off, having heard it all before. "You skated in minus seventy with only a thin layer of sparkly cloth covering your naughty bits."

That vivid description drew a laugh out of me and, to my dismay, an accompanying snort. Quickly, I covered my mouth, hoping that Gaby hadn't heard it. My snorted laugh was one of the things I'd tried to change when I completely overhauled my life, but occasionally, it still slipped out against my will.

Luck wasn't on my side, it seemed, since Gaby obviously heard me. "Very ladylike." She grinned, giving me a playful nudge. "Now come on, we've got to move!"

We half-jogged the last two blocks to the Urban Style office building. As part of our university's journalism program, Gaby and I were assigned to internships at the magazine, and that day would be our first meeting with the magazine's new editor. Rumours had been circulating that the new editor actually let interns do real work, unlike the coffee-making and photocopying we'd been stuck doing for the last two months. Desperate to get some actual writing experience, we wanted to make a good impression that day, and being late wouldn't be a great start.

Thankfully, we made it to the boardroom just in time, squeezing into a space in the corner of the rectangular room. All the regular staff had already claimed the chairs around the oval table, but we found a standing spot along the wall. As we pulled off our outerwear, I took my glasses off and rubbed them on my shirt, trying to get rid of the fog caused by the warm inside air.

"You look good without your glasses, Mia," the assistant to the editor said, peering at me from across the table. Everyone else nearby turned to look at me, and I quickly shoved the glasses back on. They completely changed the look of my face, but that was the point. Although I didn't need them to see, I got them as part of the new identity I made for myself when I moved to Toronto for university. With them on, nobody recognized me for who I used to be.

Sometimes, I barely recognized myself.

"Thanks," I mumbled before changing the subject. "Is that a new shirt, Anna? I love the colour."

My distraction worked. Everyone turned back to her, and I exhaled in relief as the spotlight on me faded.

A moment later, the chatter around the room died off as a woman in a perfectly tailored blouse and skirt walked in. In her late thirties with platinum blonde hair, cut short and perfectly sleek, she might have been mistaken for a model if we all didn't know who she was already. Samantha Pino, our new editor-in-chief, had been pretty much the sole topic of conversation around the office for the last two weeks.

"Good morning. I'm Samantha, and you can call me that. No need for formality. I'd like to know who you are and what you do at the magazine. Let's go around the room."

She wasted no time, so I kept my reply similarly brief when they got to me. "I'm Mia Wilson and I'm an intern, so I'll do anything you want me to, within reason."

A few people chuckled politely, and Samantha gave me a genuine smile. "Nice to meet you, Mia. You're at TMU?"

I nodded in confirmation. Toronto Metropolitan University had the best journalism program in the city, which was why I chose to go there. I had considered going to Carleton University in Ottawa, but moving back to Ottawa seemed like a risk. That city had too many memories and too many people who might recognize me. Starting over somewhere new felt safer.

"I'm in my third year, with Gaby," I added, pointing to my friend next to me who quickly gave her full name as well.

"Great to have you ladies with us," Samantha said before moving on to the next person.

Those few sentences were more than the previous editor-in-chief had *ever* said to me, so overall, I felt pretty pleased. Maybe luck was on my side that day after all.

Samantha outlined a few of the ideas she had for upcoming issues, and I quickly found myself getting caught up in her energy. They sounded like stories I would like to read and, even better, stories I would like to write.

One of the magazine's regular features profiled someone in the fashion industry each month, but Samantha had other ideas. "We can broaden our appeal by focusing on people in other industries. Sports, for example. I'd love to do a series profiling young, up-and-coming athletes from the city, both from a fashion perspective as well as what goes into being a top athlete."

Everyone murmured their agreement and started throwing out names of people to profile: hockey players, naturally, along with some from football, baseball, soccer, and basketball.

Gaby nudged me, and I knew exactly what she was thinking without even looking at her. Even though I shook my head, she refused to take the hint, and when I didn't speak up, she did it for me. "How about a figure skater? Those guys have great style."

Samantha nodded in approval. "Absolutely."

"Mia knows a lot of them," Gaby continued, despite the death glare I gave her. "She used to compete."

Samantha's eyebrows raised as she looked over at me. "It would be great to have someone who really understands the work that goes into what they do. What discipline did you compete in?"

With everyone's eyes on me, I tried to appear calm, though I felt far from it. "Ice dance."

Samantha's eyes lit up even further. "Perfect. Would you be interested in writing the profile, Mia?"

My mouth nearly fell open before I caught it. Writing a feature had been my dream since I started at the magazine, but interns weren't usually given anything so prominent to do. It would be a lot of pressure, but if the profile were on a skater, I wouldn't have to do that much background research. I already knew exactly what went into training. Being around the skating scene would be challenging for me, but if I wanted to excel in my new chosen career, I couldn't turn down an opportunity like this.

"Of course. I'd love to."

With a nod, Samantha made a note in her book and the conversation moved on to which of the Leafs' hockey players we should focus on. Gaby grabbed my trembling hand and squeezed it supportively, knowing as well as I did what a big opportunity I'd just been given. I definitely owed her one.

When the staff meeting finished, Gaby and I returned to our desks and got started on our other work for the day. She had the full day there, but I only had another hour before I had to return to campus for class.

Only five minutes before I had to leave, Anna walked over to us. "Mia, Samantha wants to see you in her office if you're free?"

Since I couldn't refuse a direct request from my new boss, I stood up and followed Anna to the editor-in-chief's office, where Samantha smiled up at me from her desk while Anna closed the door behind me.

"Come have a seat. I wanted to find out a bit more about you and talk about this profile that you'll be doing."

Just my luck. I didn't have time for a proper conversation, and I would have to tell her so. "I actually have to leave for class in a few minutes, but I'm so excited to get started. I already have a lot of ideas about who we could profile. Connor Adams is a singles skater with the most amazing fashion sense. He actually designs a lot of his own costumes. Or there's Patrick Evans, a pairs skater, and he's..."

Samantha held up her hands to stop the barrage of words from my mouth, chuckling to herself. "I love your enthusiasm, but I actually already have somebody in mind. My sixteen-year-old niece is usually a pretty good barometer for what's hot at any given moment, and right now, she's completely obsessed with an ice dancer named Austin Black. Do you know him?"

The name hit me like a punch to the gut for the second time that morning.

She wanted to do a profile on *Austin*?

She wanted *me* to do a profile on Austin?

The idea was ridiculous. Completely insane, actually, but I couldn't say that. After months of being stuck at the photocopier, I might not get another opportunity like this to build up my portfolio at the magazine. If I made things difficult during my very first meeting with this woman, why would she ever want to give me another chance?

On the other hand, how could I possibly agree? The idea of speaking to him made it feel like the temperature in the room had dropped thirty degrees, sending ice-cold anxiety rushing through my veins.

Despite my mouth having gone completely dry, I had to say *something* since she was waiting for a reply.

"Austin Black," I repeated, the name feeling strange in my mouth after all this time. Although I heard it from time to time, I rarely said it myself. "Yeah, he trains here in Toronto. He's... a good skater."

The obviousness of that statement made Samantha laugh. "Since he won a medal at the last world championships, I assumed as much. He's also completely gorgeous, according to my niece, but almost impossible to pin down for an interview. I tried to get him for a piece at my last magazine but it never worked out. I don't suppose you know any secret ways to get a hold of him?"

Another face immediately popped into my head, one I had tried to forget a long time ago. "His mother is the key. She loves the limelight. If we offer to feature her too, she'll get Austin to agree."

Samantha's smile filled me with both pride and dread. "That's perfect. I can already tell what a great asset to the team you are. I'm going to be assigning this whole series to Angelo to oversee, so you can get together with him tomorrow to lay out your plan of attack. How does that sound?"

Pushing down my misgivings, I did my best to look on the bright side. No one ever said being a journalist would be easy, and for my first feature byline, I would find a way to make it work. "That sounds great. Thank you so much for this opportunity, Samantha. I won't let you down."

~**Austin**~

The door to my locker slammed back against the neighboring locker as I threw it open, the clanging sound of metal echoing through the small locker room.

"Hey man, what'd that door do to you?"

Charlie, one of my training mates, laughed at me from across the room, and I did my best to push my frustration down as I ran a hand through my short hair, brushing the loose strands off my face. My bad mood wasn't Charlie's fault any more than the locker's, so snapping at him wouldn't achieve anything.

"Nothing. Guess I'm stronger than I thought."

"I don't know if it's possible to be stronger than you think you are," he teased.

"Ha ha." He wasn't as funny as he thought he was either. "Why don't you stop wasting your talents here and go into stand-up instead?"

He threw his towel at me in protest, but it fell short, landing on the ground between us, which finally did make me laugh. I guess he could be a little bit funny after all.

"Looks like someone needs more time in the weight room," I teased him right back.

A few of the other guys came in and Charlie moved on to bothering them instead, so I turned back to my locker to grab my skates. With the door open wider than usual, my eyes fell on the pictures attached to the inside of it, landing on one picture in particular: a 15-year-old girl, her hands on her hips, glaring at the camera. Glaring at *me*, really, since I'd been the one holding the camera at the time.

Somehow, five years had passed since I took that picture of my former dance partner, Amy.

After I took it, I had it printed and pinned it in my locker with a speech bubble coming from her mouth, saying, "Focus, Austin!" It had been a joke at the time, a way of teasing her for her no-nonsense attitude on the ice. She always pushed me to try more, to work harder, to take things more seriously. Not that I had ever really been a slacker, but Amy's intensity was on a whole other level when it came to our skating.

Some people found it off-putting, but I never did. I loved her passion, her drive, and her skill, and I loved to tease her and watch her little ears turn red as she tried not to let me get to her.

She failed every time.

Later, after she vanished from my life and I came to train in Toronto instead, the photo in my locker took on a whole new meaning. It became a reminder to me to never take things for granted, to appreciate the chances I was given and to make each day count.

To focus on what I wanted and what I did it all for.

As always, looking at her picture and thinking of Amy helped me put everything in perspective. I'd been angry because my mother arranged for a camera crew to come and film us on the ice that day, and she waited until just before practice to tell me about it. It frustrated me that she kept doing those kinds of things, picking and choosing which media appearances I would do and when, and generally trying to run my life as if I weren't capable of making any decisions myself.

But was it really worth getting upset about? The photo of Amy reminded me that I'd been through worse, and I could deal with it.

I could deal with anything as long as I got to keep going out there and doing what I loved every day.

With my skates laced up, I headed out to the ice, taking off my guards at the board and beginning my warm-up. I'd done the same warm-up routine for so many years, every time I stepped on the ice, that I didn't even need to think about it. I used the time to relax into the feel of the ice, to listen to my body and the way it responded to me that day, without worrying at all about the steps or what I should do next.

That day, things felt good. My body felt strong and healthy and connected to the ice. Those kinds of days were the best, and just one more thing to be grateful for.

When my personal warm-up had finished, I circled into the middle of the ice to wait for my partner, Grace. She had her own routine that she started off with but we always finished the warm-up together.

She chewed her lip as she approached. "Your mom just told me there's going to be a camera crew here today."

"Yeah, I didn't know. I'm sorry."

The media attention that naturally came with our level of competition made Grace uncomfortable. When we first started skating together, there had been a lot of unflattering comparisons made between her and Amy, my former partner, and even though that eventually faded away and only the die-hard fans remembered that I'd ever had another partner, Grace still took every comment made about her ability much more personally than she should. I tried to shield her from it when I could, but sometimes, it couldn't be helped.

For the time being, I put my arm around her to try to lift her spirits. "If we both get through this without losing it on someone, I'll take you out for gelato afterwards, okay?"

We'd discovered a gelato place in Little Italy last summer that made their own low-fat gelato, and it had become Grace's favourite guilty pleasure.

Her shoulders relaxed as she smiled up at me. "I'd love that, Austin."

"Good. Then let's skate."

~**Amelia**~

After my class finished, I made my way to the cafeteria for dinner where Gaby met me along with Rosa and Jenna, two other friends from our journalism program. We had barely sat down before Gaby announced my new assignment to the others.

"You get to write a feature article for the magazine?" Jenna repeated incredulously. "That's amazing. All I've gotten to write so far in my internship is a sign to tell people not to touch the food in the fridge."

"Let's focus on the more important thing," Rosa interjected. "You get to follow a hot male athlete around? Like, in the locker room?"

Rosa always chose to focus on the opposite gender given any opportunity to do so. The girl had a one-track mind.

"That's actually the problem," I admitted, and three curious faces turned towards me.

"Why is it a problem?" Gaby asked, just as clueless as the others since I hadn't had a chance to tell her about my conversation with Samantha yet. She knew about the article, but not who I had to write about.

That meant I got to drop the bomb on them all at the same time. "They want me to profile Austin."

As I expected, their jaws all hit the floor.

"Austin?" Jenna gasped. "Your ex-skating partner Austin?"

"Jerk-who-abandoned-you Austin?" Gaby's protectiveness shone through, as usual.

"Love-of-your-life Austin?" That came from Rosa, of course.

"Yes, that Austin." My head fell into my hands as I answered them all. "What am I going to do? I don't know if he'll talk to me, and even if he does, I don't know if I should do it. I mean: is it a conflict of interest?"

"I don't think it is," Gaby replied. "Just because you used to know the guy doesn't mean you're going to be biased. You can write the feature impartially. That's what being a professional journalist is all about."

"But what if he doesn't think so?" The idea of talking to Austin again after all this time made my stomach churn. "What if he refuses to talk to me?"

"Does he need to know it's you?" Jenna suggested in response. "I mean, would he even recognize you?"

Rosa rolled her eyes. "Of course he would recognize her. They skated together for three years. It's not like she met him once at the mall."

"Actually..." Gaby countered, trailing off for a second as we all looked over at her. Her fingers drummed on the dining table as she thought it over before inviting us aboard her train of thought. "He might not recognize you if you really try to hide it. I've seen the pictures of you and Austin from back then. You're taller now, you've straightened and dyed your hair, you started wearing glasses. I bet you even sound different if you really lean into your Newfoundland accent. Plus, you changed your name! He doesn't know you as Mia. It's been four years. Maybe he wouldn't know it's you."

As ridiculous as it sounded, Gaby had a point. The guy I had been in love with for all my teenage years had never noticed me when I was right in front of him. Why would he pay any attention to me now?

I couldn't exactly go in disguise, but I could sort of go undercover. Wear lots of layers, keep my face hidden behind my glasses and my new bangs. I'd spent two years living with my mom in St John's before moving to Toronto, and I *had* picked up a bit of the accent. I could play it up a bit. Maybe it would be enough to throw him off.

It sounded crazy, but it might work.

Austin had a new rink, a new coach, a new partner, a whole new life. Nobody else there would know me, and it wasn't like he'd been thinking of me every day for the past four years, not like I'd been thinking of him.

Reaching down, I ran my fingers over my four-leaf clover necklace, the one he had given me. Maybe, with a little luck, I might actually be able to pull it off.

Chapter Two

~**Austin**~

"Stop!"

Brian's frustrated voice called to us from the boards, and all the forward momentum Grace and I had built fizzled out. The tension in our bodies slackened, and we glided together towards our coach to get his feedback, her hand still holding mine.

"It's still not right. Grace, you need to make the turn out of the rocker faster or the twizzles won't be in sync. Try it again."

Grace hung her head, breathing heavily, and I gave her hand an encouraging squeeze. I didn't blame her at all. We'd been working on this circular step sequence for half the session, and it didn't feel right to me either.

Unfortunately, that was as much as I could say about it. I knew when things felt natural on the ice and when they didn't, but I'd never been great at understanding why or figuring out how to improve it. That had always been my old partner Amy's strong suit. Whenever something felt off, she would immediately understand exactly what part of the movement to blame for it, and she would usually suggest something ten times better to take its place.

Grace didn't have that skill any more than I did, so all we could do was trust our choreographer and do our best to make it work.

After running through it three more times, we were more in unison even if it still didn't feel completely right to either of us. The choreographer assured us it just needed more practice. Once we were used to it, it would feel more natural, he assured us.

Grabbing my guards and a towel from the side of the rink, I hopped off the ice and headed towards the locker room.

"Hey, Austin?" Grace called out from behind me, stumbling slightly as she put her own guards on while trying to keep up with me.

"Yeah?"

"I just wanted to say thanks again for the gelato last night." She smiled up at me as she spoke. "It was nice to just hang out for a bit, just the two of us."

"Sure," I agreed. "No problem. I'll see you tomorrow."

I turned back towards the locker room, but she stopped me again. "I was wondering if you had plans for supper tonight?"

Damn it. My eyes closed for a moment with my back still to her, but after putting a forced smile on my face, I turned back to her. "I'm just heading home. I'll probably have an early night since we've got the early ice time tomorrow. I'll see you then, okay?"

She reached out to stop me that time, placing a hand on my arm. "I could come over," she offered. "I can cook us something."

"No, thanks," I declined, still smiling to try to soften the refusal. "Not tonight. See you later, Grace."

Finally, she let me go and I escaped to the locker room, throwing myself down on the bench in frustration. I should have known that taking Grace out the previous evening would be a bad idea. I wanted to make up for the whole surprise camera thing my mom arranged, but clearly, Grace read more into it than that.

It had been a couple of months since I started to realize she might be hoping for a closer relationship between us off the ice. I'd never encouraged her, but it didn't help that just about everyone else in the world already thought we were dating. Our coach thought it didn't hurt for us to seem like a couple, so that whenever we did romantic or sensual programs, the judges and the audience would find it believable. Whenever we were asked about our relationship status, we were supposed to deflect the question, not answering definitively one way or the other.

Since neither of us were dating anyone else seriously, it didn't seem like a big deal. I didn't particularly like doing it, but at least I thought we were both on the same page, that we both understood it was just for show.

I thought that right up until she tried to kiss me at a friend's birthday party a couple of months ago. I stopped her before anything really happened, and she swore afterwards that she'd only done it because she'd been drinking. However, after that, I started to notice lots of little things that I never paid attention to before.

The way she held onto my hand on the ice even when we were just talking to our coach. How she'd always make sure to save me a place next to her at the cafeteria between sessions. How she'd always be interested in the same movies or concerts I was whenever we chatted with our other friends at the club about things to do over the weekend.

I tried to make it clear that we were only friends and I thought I'd done a decent job of it without being too harsh. When we had to work together every day, hurting her feelings wouldn't help anything, and I knew from experience that mixing a professional partnership with personal feelings didn't necessarily end well.

Hopefully, she would take the hint and that would be the end of it. I really, really hoped so. The last thing I wanted was for anything to mess up all the work that Grace and I had put into getting to where we were. Not when we were so close to getting everything we'd ever wanted.

~Amelia~

The day after I got the assignment to profile Austin, I met with the magazine's features editor, Angelo, to discuss my plans on how to approach it. I'd lain awake half the night, weighing all my options in my head.

First, I tried to reconcile the potential conflict of interest. If I told Angelo about my past relationship with Austin, he might decide to give the feature to someone else and I would lose this amazing opportunity, which I really didn't want to happen. Gaby said I could be impartial, and I believed I could be too. Painting Austin in a bad light wouldn't benefit me in any way, but I wouldn't give him a free pass either. I could be professional and treat him like any other random person I might be profiling.

However, that would only work if *he* treated *me* like any other reporter. If Austin knew I was the one interviewing him, he might not talk to me at all, and even if he did, our own past could overshadow everything else. It would be too much of a distraction.

The more I thought about it, the more convinced I became that my only option, if I wanted to do the article, would be to keep my past identity hidden from everyone, including Austin.

That was the decision I made by the time I spoke to Angelo, and it felt like the right one. He seemed to have some concerns about having an intern write the piece in the first place, quizzing me on my process and previous experience, and if I told him my other concerns, he probably would have pulled the plug immediately.

So, I didn't mention that I knew Austin. Instead, I spent the time in our meeting going over the ideas I had about shadowing Austin to get a personal view of him, and the kind of photos we could take to enhance the article.

"This is good work," he conceded when he finished reviewing the outline I'd put together. "Samantha mentioned you plan to reach out to him through his mother?"

"That's right. I thought we could do an accompanying column about fashion among the parents who spend their time in the rink supporting their kids. If we include a picture or two of her in it, she'll jump at the chance."

"Appeal to both generations," Angelo concluded with a nod. "Sounds good. I'll assign a photographer to work with you. The sooner we can get started, the better."

Flush with the victory of his agreement, I returned to my desk, determined to get started before I lost my nerve. The first step would be to contact Austin's mother.

Assuming she still had the same cell number she'd had four years ago, that shouldn't be too difficult. My mom would have that number, so I gave her a call.

"Hi, sweetheart," she greeted me with a smile in her voice. "This is a nice surprise."

We usually only spoke on the weekends, so calling during the week was out of the ordinary, and I jumped straight to the reason for my call. "I actually need a favour. It's something for school."

I phrased it that way on purpose. She'd been the biggest supporter of me moving on with my life and pursuing a new career, so anything I needed for school, she would give me.

"Of course," she agreed readily, as I expected. "What is it?"

Despite her response, I knew she wouldn't like the actual request, so I took a deep breath to steady myself before I said the words. "I need Mrs Black's phone number. Austin's mom."

The silence on the other end of the phone lasted so long that I began to wonder if the call had dropped.

"Mom?" I prompted. "Can you hear me?"

"Why do you want to talk to her?" Suspicion and concern surrounded the question, and I couldn't really blame her. Mrs Black had never been anything other than horrible to both of us, and the idea of talking to her didn't appeal to me any more than it did to my mother.

However, it would be my best chance of getting to Austin, so I had to try. As succinctly as I could, I explained the article and my plan to hide my true identity from Austin.

That part seemed to make her feel a bit better. "You're really not going to tell him who you are?"

"No," I assured her. "That would just complicate things, and I'm sure he doesn't want to see me anyway. I need to interview him for the article, and that's it."

She sighed, still not sounding fully convinced, but when I reminded her what a boost this could be for my fledgling career, she relented. "This is the last number I had for her. Just be careful, okay, Mia? I know how difficult the whole thing was for you and I don't want you getting hurt again."

I assured her I would be extremely careful, and promised I would keep her updated on how it went.

Armed with Mrs Black's last-known number, I punched it into the phone, trying to ignore the way my hand shook as I held the phone to my ear. I fully expected the call to go to voicemail, if the number still worked at all, so when she actually answered, it caught me completely off guard.

"Yes?"

That one word in her clipped, assured tone made me instantly feel thirteen years old again. I could still hear her at the boards the first time I had skated with Austin.

"Is that the best she can do? We're wasting our time here."

I paused a second too long, and she hung up.

Damn it. I quickly redialed and that time, it did go to voicemail. At least I'd prepared for that, and with my eyes on the script in front of me, I played up my accent just enough that my voice would be unrecognizable.

"Mrs Black, my name is Mia Wilson, I'm calling from Urban Style magazine. We're interested in doing a feature on Austin for an upcoming issue, and our photographer is also interested in capturing the latest rink-side fashions. It's no secret that you're one of the best-dressed women at any competition, so if it's convenient for you, we'd like to do photo shoots for you and Austin at the same time, as well as a series of short interviews with Austin. All at the rink, naturally, so he doesn't miss any training time. If you would be interested in discussing this further, please give me a call at 416-555-8923. Thank you."

As soon as I hung up, I exhaled a long breath, feeling pretty sure I'd managed to get all the words out and in the right order, even though the memory of her snapped "Yes?" sent a shiver down my spine. Hopefully, this article would be worth any time spent in her presence. Not seeing her anymore had been the one good thing about my partnership with Austin ending.

He had such a huge blind spot when it came to his mother. Everyone else saw how controlling and manipulative she could be, but he always downplayed it, focusing on the sacrifices she'd made for him. She *had* made sacrifices, all of our parents did, but it always felt like hers had been as much for herself as for Austin. She wanted the prestige that came with being the mother of a champion, and now, she had it. That should have made her happy, but from that one word I'd heard, it didn't seem like success had mellowed her out at all.

My phone rang while still in my hand, making me jump, and I almost couldn't believe the call display when Mrs Black's name came up. "H-hello?" I answered, wincing at my stammered greeting.

The pause on the other end seemed unimpressed too, and a moment later, Mrs Black's unmistakable voice rang in my ear. "Ms Wilson?"

Steeling my nerves, I answered more forcefully. "Yes, this is Mia Wilson. Thank you for calling me back so quickly."

"I got your message and I'm interested in hearing more about your proposal. I have a list of conditions for any interviews with Austin, and I'll need background information on the magazine and you, Ms Wilson. Send me an email and we can discuss the details."

She rattled off her email address and hung up before I could say anything else. In spite of her rudeness, the exchange actually made me smile. Some things never changed, it seemed: Austin's mother was the same as she had always been.

I sent Mrs Black an email as she requested, keeping my own biography as brief as possible. I sent her a couple of articles I'd done for our school's paper, and I explained that I had a background in figure skating and understood the sport. I assured her I wouldn't ask any uninformed questions.

She replied later that evening with her list of conditions, which were more for her benefit than for Austin's, I couldn't help noticing. All contact would go through her. She'd have final approval of all photos and copy.

I sent them on to Angelo to ask for his input since he would have far more experience than I did dealing with things like this. Only one condition really made me pause: under topics that were off limits for interview questions, it listed 'former skating partners.'

I knew Austin never talked about me in his interviews and it never really surprised me. He had moved on, so why dwell on the past? However, I hadn't had any idea that reporters weren't even allowed to *ask* about me. Was working with me really that horrible a memory for him?

At least if he didn't want to talk about it, it would make it easy for me to avoid the subject, which meant less of a chance of me revealing anything that might disclose my actual identity. As much as I didn't understand why he had that condition at all, it would actually work in my favour.

Angelo helped me to iron out all the details with Mrs Black and we made arrangements for the photo shoot and the first interview with Austin. After that, I planned to speak to him directly to determine the best times for me to shadow him. I had no intention of going through Mrs Black again unless I absolutely had to.

As I looked over my notes, I wondered how much his schedule had changed since I was a daily part of it. How much had *he* changed?

Ready or not, I was about to find out.

~**Austin**~

The day started normally enough. As always, I got up at six o'clock and did a yoga session in my home gym, had a shower, made myself breakfast and drove over to the rink.

There, I met up with Charlie and we ran through our calisthenics program: squats, sit-ups, pull-ups, abdominal exercises and more. Charlie and I usually tried to do the routine together a few times a week so we could talk to each other and distract ourselves from the grueling workout.

"You missed a good time at Angela's on Saturday," he told me as we started on a series of lunges. Sweat trickled down my back as I worked the thigh muscles which needed to power me around the ice. "Grace asked about you."

That was exactly why I *didn't* go. One of the other ice dancers invited a bunch of us over for drinks after training, and normally, I'd be happy for a relaxed night out when we didn't have training the next day.

However, Grace looked so eager when she asked if I planned to go that I decided to skip it.

"Are you sure you don't want to try dating a girl for a change?" I asked him, only half-joking. "You could go out with her."

Charlie laughed. "Come on, she's not that bad. You're not seeing anyone else and she's clearly into you. Why not have some fun?"

"Because I have to work with her every day," I reminded him. "And I'm just not attracted to her. She's like my sister."

"Your sister who has a huge crush on you."

Charlie laughed again as I rolled my eyes back at him. We both got down on the floor to do some crunches while I tried to further explain my reluctance. "There are enough fangirls out there who think they're in love with me. I don't need it from my partner too."

"Oh, your life is so hard." Charlie laughed even harder before putting on a high-pitched voice in what I assumed was meant to be an imitation of me. "Everybody loves me, I don't ever get a minute to myself."

"Shut up," I grumbled, poking him in the ribs in the middle of his sit-up.

"Ow!" He rubbed his chest where I'd poked him, and his face fell. "Man, now I've lost count. I have to start over."

I started again with him by way of apology. "Look, I'm not saying everyone's in love with me. I'm just tired of people thinking they know me because they've seen me on TV and read a few things about me. And I'm tired of Grace not taking no for an answer."

"I think you just want someone who's going to make you work for it," Charlie suggested. "You've got all these girls throwing themselves at you, but you want to be the one doing the chasing."

He might have a point there, though I would never admit it to him. "Whereas you only want the boys who throw themselves at you."

His grin spread from ear to ear. "Hey, if they're going to jump right in the net, who am I to complain?"

We finished the rest of our workout talking about Charlie's love life instead of mine, which was fine by me. After a cool-down, I headed over to the showers for another quick wash before getting ready to get on the ice.

~Amelia~

Butterflies fluttered in my stomach as soon as I woke up and remembered that I would be seeing Austin that day. After all these years, all the glimpses of him on TV and in newspapers and online, I would finally see him again in person.

A day that could lead to the biggest story of my fledgling career, or one that could end in disaster.

Only one thing made sense to start a day like that.

I had to go skating.

When I first moved to Toronto, I touched base with Terry, an old family friend who had been one of my biggest fans when I skated. I asked him if he knew where I could get some ice time to keep myself in shape, and his weathered face lit up. It turned out that in his retirement, he drove the Zamboni at a rink not too far from the university. It worked out so well, I might have called it fate if I still believed in such a thing.

Ever since, he let me tag along with him early in the morning when he opened the rink, to have half an hour to myself on the ice before he flooded it for the first hockey practice of the day. Four or five times a week, depending on his schedule and mine, we would catch up as I changed into my skates, chatting about my school work, his grandkids or the latest news.

All of that faded away as soon I opened the door in the boards. The moment my blade connected with the ice, the only thing that existed for me was the way my body moved and the electricity that flowed through me as I skated.

Terry sat in the stands and watched me while he drank his coffee, even if I only practiced my stroking or figures. He told me it was his favourite part of the day.

It was my favourite part of the day too.

That morning, I cued up an old piece of music on my phone, for a dance I hadn't done in a very long time. At least, I hadn't done it on the ice; in my head, I performed it regularly, and even more often in my dreams. On the ice, though, I only felt Austin's absence. Without him, it didn't feel right.

However, that day, when I knew I would see him for the first time in four years, I wanted to try it again. I wanted to feel connected, not with Austin necessarily, but with the girl I had been the last time I saw him.

The girl I had been before everything went wrong for me.

If I closed my eyes, I could almost feel his hand in mine, his arm around my back and his strong body pressed against me. Instead of avoiding the memories as I usually did, I leaned into them, pouring my heart into the dance that we had never got to perform the way we wanted to.

When I got off the ice, Terry had tears in his eyes. "You should be in front of stadiums, Amy. Stadiums full of cheering crowds, not just me and the Zamboni."

He always called me Amy. Most people who knew me from my previous life had adjusted to calling me Mia, but Terry could never seem to remember and I didn't bother to correct him. It took all my energy just to keep from crying myself, he looked so proud. "You're the best audience I could ever ask for. Same time tomorrow? I'll bring you some TimBits."

"You always know the way to my heart." Lines crinkled around his eyes as he smiled. The doughnut holes were his favourite treat. "Enjoy the rest of your day. Are you doing anything exciting?"

I hadn't mentioned seeing Austin, and I couldn't bring myself to say his name then either. "Just working on a story for the magazine," I said, not technically lying.

After promising Terry I could bring him a copy of the magazine when my story got published, I changed back to my shoes and jogged back to my dorm. Although it was still only 6:30 and the meeting with Austin at the rink wasn't scheduled until 11, I started to get ready right away. No point in leaving anything to chance.

Taking my time, I showered and blew out my hair. Once blonde, naturally curly and almost always pulled back in a tight bun, it was now black and straightened, framing my face with thick bangs. Rather than the heavy make-up I used to wear for competition, my foundation and blush were subtle, with the effective use of some eyeliner to help alter the shape of my eyes. I shaded in my eyebrows, making them thicker than they used to be, and my thick-rimmed chunky glasses covered nearly half my face, from the bottom of my bangs to the middle of my cheeks.

The clothes I chose would be important too. Unlike the tight, stretchy clothes I wore back when I skated, I went with a professional look: a black skirt with black tights and a pink blouse. They matched my black hair and glasses perfectly.

Lastly, I tucked my four-leaf clover necklace safely inside my blouse. I couldn't bear not to wear my good-luck charm on a day when I needed luck more than ever, but I didn't want anyone to see it either. *Especially* Austin.

When I'd finished, I scrutinized myself in the full-length mirror, trying to see myself through Austin's eyes. Was there anything that might give away my identity? Any part of Amy that he might recognize?

I honestly didn't think so. Short of getting plastic surgery, I'd changed my appearance as much as possible over the past four years. The girl I'd been back when he knew me wouldn't have recognized the woman in the mirror, so there was no reason he should either.

Satisfied with my cover-up, I put on my black slouch boots and my matching puffy coat, grabbed my portable recorder and my notepad, and headed for the door.

I could do this. For the sake of my first big magazine assignment, I *would* do it. I would treat it like any other interview and any other interview subject, keeping myself out of the story.

It had just passed ten o'clock when I arrived at the skating club, but I didn't mind being early. It beat being late, and besides, being there early gave me a chance to take a look around and familiarize myself with the facilities. I'd never been to that particular club before. Austin moved to Toronto to train when he switched coaches, right after he found his new partner. I'd never met Grace Matthews, but I probably would at some point during the interview process, and I needed to be ready for that too.

From seeing her on TV, I knew she was older than me, and that she was Austin's girlfriend as well as his partner. My stomach twisted at the thought, no matter how much I told myself that jealousy was ridiculous. He hadn't been my partner in years, and he had never been my boyfriend. Who he dated made no difference to me.

Except that the magazine's readers would want the question asked, which meant I would have to find a way to bring it up even though I really didn't want to.

After I checked in with security and they pointed me in the direction of the rink where Austin and Grace trained, I wandered around the public areas, checking out the gym and therapy areas in particular. Hopefully, Austin would show me which of the facilities he made use of in his training regimen. A lot of people thought that skaters did all of their work on the ice, but there was a lot more to it than that.

The thought of walking around and talking with him made my stomach flutter yet again, but I pushed my nerves down as firmly as I could. There was no going back now.

Looking for the entrance to the rink viewing area, I pushed the long metal bar to open another door and began making my way down another small hallway. Halfway down the hall, a familiar voice drifted out from behind a half-open door and stopped me in my tracks.

Austin's mom had always had a voice that carried, and though I knew I should probably keep going, I found myself creeping closer to the door instead to hear what she had to say.

~Austin~

Halfway through getting changed into my training clothes, the door to the locker room swung open and my mom strolled in.

"I told you to knock first," I reminded her, quickly turning around as I finished pulling up my track pants. "The other guys don't appreciate you just walking in."

That was an understatement. My training mates had several nicknames for my mother based on her tendency to show up anywhere and everywhere as if the whole rink belonged to her. None of them were flattering.

My mom brushed my objections away with a wave of her hand. "There's no one else in here. And even if there was, it's nothing I haven't seen before."

Gritting my teeth, I pushed away the discomforting image those words conjured. Arguing wouldn't do me any good. The year before, at the age of twenty-two, I finally managed to convince her to let me move out on my own, but she remained my self-appointed publicist and manager, showing up at the rink nearly every day. My career was her whole life, so even though the other skaters didn't like her hanging around all the time, I didn't know how I could stop her. If I knew how to get her to back off without hurting her feelings, I'd have done it a long time ago.

"What do you need?" I asked, trying to move her along before any of the other guys showed up.

Her reply made me groan in frustration. "I forgot to tell you there's a girl from a magazine coming to do an interview with you today."

Seriously? After the camera crew the week before, she wanted to spring *another* media thing on me? She had a habit of 'forgetting' to tell me so that I never had a chance to say no. It would make me look like a jerk if I refused to talk to someone when they were already there.

"I told you I didn't want any more people here at the rink while we're training."

She had clearly anticipated my reluctance because she kept on talking. "You just have to be polite and let her follow you around for a bit. She's a big skating fan, apparently, so she'll be thrilled just to talk to you. It won't do you any harm."

A fan? That sounded even worse. "I don't need any more distractions, especially from a fangirl who convinced some magazine to send her here."

"It won't be a distraction," my mom assured me. "I'll keep her busy and just bring her down at the end of the session to ask you a question or two. They'll take a few photos, and that's it. Ten minutes, tops."

"Fine," I snapped, knowing that I really didn't have a choice. "But I don't want her bothering Grace."

Grace often got annoyed with the way some of our female fans threw themselves at me. She said the annoyance was on my behalf, but I suspected jealousy also played a role, and with the current situation between us, some random woman stirring the pot where Grace was concerned would be the last thing I needed.

"I'll take care of everything," my mom said, her voice taking on the soothing, cajoling tone she used when she wanted something from me. "Just wear something nice for the photos."

I'd wear what I always wore, but I didn't bother arguing with her. "I'll see you out there."

When she left, I took a deep breath to refocus and got back to getting ready for my session. Our first competition of the year was coming up and the last thing I needed was another distraction, not from my mother and definitely not from some girl from a magazine.

~**Amelia**~

My heart raced as I set off back the way I came, hardly able to believe what I just heard. Austin had no idea I was coming. His mother hadn't asked him if he wanted to do the article or even told him about it until right that moment, and then she told him he only had to give me ten minutes.

What the hell? A full-length feature piece required a lot more than a question or two, and I made my request to shadow him clear when I emailed her. His tone of voice told me he didn't want to be doing it at all, and to add insult to injury, his mother just gave him the impression that I was an obsessed fan who had a crush on him.

All of that had my heart pounding, but it didn't fully explain the painfully hard thumping against my ribs. Part of it also had to do with the sound of Austin's voice and the way it moved straight through me, from the top of my head to the tip of my toes. That voice in my ear as we danced had been one of the things I liked most about him, and somehow, it sounded even sexier than I remembered. How was that even possible?

Back in the rink's lobby, I found a quiet spot to catch my breath and calm myself. Things weren't going the way I hoped, but as a skater, I knew that if you stumbled, you couldn't just quit. You had to finish the program. Running away wasn't an option, so after giving myself a minute to collect my thoughts, I squared my shoulders and headed to the entrance where Paul, the magazine's photographer, had just arrived.

"Hey, Mia," he greeted me, giving me a cheerful smile. A few years older than me and amazing with a camera, Paul was also friendly and easygoing, the perfect companion for my first piece. I'd been really excited to learn he'd been assigned to help me.

I tried to give him a genuine smile in return and not let on that anything might be wrong. "Hi. I'm just about to head to the rink. Do you want to come and take a look at the best place to set up for some action shots?"

He readily agreed and we headed off to the practice ice, using a different entrance than the one I had just tried. It led to the stands rather than the locker rooms, and the moment we stepped through the doorway, Mrs Black appeared directly in front of us, like something out of my nightmares. Her platinum blonde hair, perfectly styled as if she had just come from the salon, her expensive designer clothes, and the fake smile on her face were all exactly as I remembered them. My skin crawled at the sight of her, especially after the exchange I just overheard between her and Austin, but she didn't even glance in my direction.

"You must be the photographer with Urban Style," she guessed, offering her hand to Paul. As he had a large, professional camera slung around his neck, it was an educated guess. "I'm Cynthia Black, delighted to meet you."

Paul shot me a quick look that I interpreted as 'what the hell?', but he took Mrs Black's hand anyway and shook it. "That's right, Mrs Black, I'm Paul Miller and this is Mia Wilson. She's the one doing the profile."

Despite his obvious attempt to give me control over the situation, Mrs Black took no notice of his efforts, exactly as I would have predicted. "Call me Cynthia, please." She linked her arm through his and continued to ignore me entirely as she pulled him along. "I have eight different outfits here for our shoot, I think you'll find the lighting is best over here..."

Paul looked back over his shoulder at me and I gave him an apologetic shrug. As bad as I felt about abandoning him, I had no desire to spend any time with Mrs Black that I didn't have to. Hopefully, he could get her photos out of the way and we could focus on getting some shots of Austin, the reason we were actually there.

The Zamboni on the ice had just finished its flood, so I wandered over to the rink boards to get a feel for the session. A small group of skaters hovered by the door to the ice, waiting for the signal to get back on. Neither Austin nor Grace were among them, but as soon as the door swung open and the eager skaters spilled onto the ice, Austin appeared.

Every nerve of my body instantly felt more alert, setting me on edge as adrenaline flooded my body, and I forced myself to look away. He didn't need to catch me staring. After the things his mother had said, it would only make me seem like more of a stalker. Instead, I kept my eyes on the ice as the skaters spread out over the ice to begin their warm-ups. I watched their skates rather than their faces, my ears filled with the familiar swish of the blades cutting through the ice. A young pair came down the ice, doing a few twizzles as part of their warm up, and I leaned a bit further over the boards to watch the patterns they left in their wake.

Suddenly, a gust of wind blew me back as my nose came within inches of a muscular arm. Holding on to the boards to steady myself, I barely managed to keep my balance, while on the ice, the perpetrator didn't even slow down. He continued his lazy strokes around the rink, and my stomach flipped as I realized who it was and what he was doing.

Austin always started his on-ice warm-up that way, with long, steady strokes right around the edge of the ice. Every movement looked utterly familiar, and completely new at the same time. Now that I'd looked, I couldn't take my eyes off him.

His dark hair was still cut short, as it always had been, but if anything, he'd grown even more handsome in the years since I'd last seen him. His features were sharper somehow, more defined, and a shadow of stubble traced a line along his jaw. His lean, muscular limbs radiated power as he moved, his speed effortless and the way he carried himself both elegant and natural.

To my horror, tears sprang to my eyes as memories crowded in, and I took several more steps back, urging myself to calm down. No. No, no, no. I was *not* going to cry. This day wouldn't start in tears. I wouldn't let it.

"Everything okay?" Paul's voice asked from behind me.

Blinking away the moisture in my eyes, I turned to him with a forced smile. "Yeah, of course. What happened to your model?"

Mrs Black was nowhere in sight, and Paul rolled his eyes. Apparently, he'd already come to the same opinion of her that most people held. "She's getting changed into the first of her many outfits. How many photos do we need of this woman?"

My lips twisted into an apologetic grimace. "Only one. Maybe two if we've got extra space to fill. Sorry."

He sighed, but seemed to accept his fate. "At least she told me I could take some photos of your guy while she's between costumes. That's him in the black there?" He pointed in Austin's direction and I nodded. Paul snapped a couple of photos in quick succession as a test before lowering the camera to check his settings.

The camera attracted Austin's attention, and the next thing I knew, he headed in our direction, a frown on his handsome face.

With a deep breath, I prepared myself to come face-to-face with my former partner for the first time in years.

Time to make a good first impression.

Chapter Three

~**Austin**~

Just as I finished my individual warm-up and headed to the centre of the ice to wait for Grace to join me, I noticed the guy on the far side of the ice, his camera pointed at me. It must have been someone from the magazine my mom mentioned, but she didn't say anything about taking pictures during practice, only at the end of the session.

Frustration bubbled up inside me, only partly because of the camera. Most of it came from being really tired of everyone assuming what I would be okay with or what I wanted without talking to me first. Before I even realized what I meant to do, my feet had started pushing me over to the guy with the camera.

"You mind asking me before you start taking photos?" I demanded, planting my hands firmly on the boards in front of him. My words came out with a jagged edge, more sharply than the situation needed, to be honest, but I couldn't seem to help it. After everything my mother had pulled, this was the last straw.

The guy's eyebrows raised, surprised by the question or my tone, or both. "Sorry. Your mother said she'd cleared it with you."

Of course she did. "My mother doesn't speak for me. If you want something from me, ask me directly."

"Of course. We will, Mr Black. We didn't mean to disturb your training."

Those words didn't come from the guy with the camera, but a woman standing next to him. I hadn't even noticed her there, but she must be the one writing the article, the fan my mother mentioned, so I turned to get a look at her.

Thick-rimmed glasses covered her eyes, with dark hair framing and partially concealing her face. Her body had been bundled up in so many layers, she wouldn't have been out of place on an Arctic expedition. Nothing about her appearance should have been particularly appealing, but as our eyes connected, a vibration thrummed through my whole body, taking me completely by surprise.

What the hell was that about?

Something about her seemed familiar, like I should know her, but I felt equally sure we hadn't met before. Surely I would remember if we had.

Her eyes widened as we stared at each other, letting me see their light blue colour a little better, and I couldn't help wondering if she felt the strange current that seemed to pass between us too. I'd never felt anything quite like it.

"I'm Mia Wilson," she introduced herself after a moment's pause, her voice lilting with a melodic Newfoundland accent. "This is Paul Miller. We're from Urban Style magazine."

Right. The magazine. The photos. I'd nearly forgotten. "You want to take pictures during our training?"

"Yes," she confirmed, smiling up at the guy with the camera in a way that set off a twinge of discomfort in my chest, for no good reason I could think of.

I didn't want to make any decisions for Grace, the same way that I wouldn't appreciate her making them for me. "I'll check with my partner."

The girl winced at my words, and I had no idea what would have caused that reaction, no more than I understood my own reactions. The whole interaction was very strange, and I skated off before things could get any weirder.

Grace stood in the centre of the ice, waiting for me as I headed back there. "Who's that?" she asked, looking past me towards the two people I had just been speaking to, and I realized I'd forgotten their names already. The woman had told me what they were, but I'd been too distracted by the way I felt to pay attention.

I stuck to the basics of why they were there instead. "They're with a magazine and are doing a story on me. They want to take some pictures of us training. Is that okay with you?"

She gave me a curious look, knowing I didn't like any distractions while we worked. "Is it okay with *you?*"

Not wanting to admit that I didn't want to say no to the woman, I shrugged. The fact that I didn't want to say no to her was crazy, since we just met and I didn't know anything about her, but that didn't make it any less true.

"I'll go have a quick chat with them," Grace offered. Before I could object, she made her way over to them, leaving me standing alone in the middle of the ice, not quite sure what to do with myself next.

~Amelia~

That didn't go exactly to plan, but I still counted it as a success overall. Austin seemed pretty annoyed when he came over, but thankfully, he calmed down quickly. Most importantly, he didn't appear to recognize me at all.

There was one moment when I got worried, the moment he looked over at me for the first time. As his eyes widened, I thought I saw a flicker of recognition. My heart began to race as my mind scrambled for a way to explain what I was doing there. However, just as quickly, the look fell away, and I realized I must have imagined it.

He really didn't recognize me.

Relief flooded through me, accompanied by a tiny ripple of disappointment. Which was stupid, since I didn't *want* him to recognize me, but some small part of me must have hoped he would anyway.

Hoped that he hadn't forgotten all about me after all.

Even more stupid was the twinge of jealousy I felt when he referred to Grace as his partner. I hadn't been his partner for four years, so what did I expect him to call her? It hadn't occurred to me that it would bother me, but it did anyway, and my lack of control over my emotions frustrated me.

Paul and I watched as Austin skated back over to Grace, they exchanged a few words, and soon, she skated over to us, a bright smile on her face. Dressed for training rather than a performance, she looked even prettier than she did with her heavy makeup on TV, and my chest tightened again as I imagined the two of them hanging out together, going on dates, and doing all the things Austin and I never did.

"Hi there," she said, her eyes on me rather than Paul. "I'm Grace. You guys are here to do a story on Austin?"

I nodded, more confused than ever. In the dressing room, Austin told his mother he didn't want me talking to Grace, so why would he send her over? At a loss, I simply introduced us again. "I'm Mia, and this is Paul. Paul's going to take a few photos while you're working, and I'll speak to Austin when you're done. We don't want to disturb your practice, so please, pretend we aren't here."

"Sounds good," she said, the smile staying on her face while she spoke. "Nice to meet you Mia, Paul."

Briefly, I wondered if the friendliness was for real or an act, but I quickly shut down that line of thought. I had no reason to be cynical or catty when it came to Grace. She hadn't done anything wrong, and I couldn't blame her for the way I felt. Until given a reason to think otherwise, I should give her the benefit of the doubt.

She skated back over to Austin and said something to him which made his shoulders relax. Their hands slid naturally into each other's grasp and they started skating around the rink together, their strokes perfectly synchronized as they began their joint warm-up.

A couple of minutes later, Mrs Black reappeared in the first of her fashion choices and Paul left me to take some photos of her. With my notebook, I took a seat in the stands and tried to swallow the lump in my throat as my eyes followed Austin and Grace around the rink. Watching his hand holding Grace's, I could almost feel his palm against mine and the way it felt to be at his side, as we made deep edges in the ice, our bodies moving exactly in sync.

This was going to be a lot harder than I thought.

Hoping to distract myself, I turned my attention to my notes and the questions that I'd jotted down to ask Austin for the profile. I didn't want the interview to be too formal, but after hearing him with his mother and after the tense way he spoke to us earlier, I couldn't be sure what to expect. Hopefully, if we made it through the rest of the practice session without causing any more disruptions, he'd be in a better mood by the end.

Austin and Grace started work on one of their pattern dances for the year, the Rhumba. The pattern dances were set dances that all dancers performed so I knew them well, and the Rhumba had always been one of my favourites. Sitting in my seat, my feet completed the steps right along with them, though I barely realized they were moving.

"Maybe you should have brought your skates."

Paul's teasing voice cut through my concentration, and I blushed.

"I didn't see you there," I mumbled.

"Obviously." He laughed as he sat down next to me. "Did you use to skate?"

"Yeah. It's been a while, but I know this dance."

"Tell me about it," Paul invited. Since he sounded genuinely interested, I ran him through the steps as Austin and Grace completed them, pointing out when they were doing it particularly well.

When they completed the choctaw sequence, however, I frowned. Something looked off.

Their coach saw it too, and he called them over to the boards. Subconsciously, I leaned forward in my seat, wishing I were closer so I could hear what he said.

Reading my mind, Paul gestured down the rink to where the coaches stood and gave me a knowing smile. "That looks like a good place to grab a photo from. You want to come with me?"

Accepting with a grateful smile, I followed him along the boards, closer to the coaching team. Mrs Black had returned to the rink as well, in yet another outfit, but her attention wasn't on Paul at the moment. She stood beside the coach, watching the ice intently and listening to everything the coach said.

Sticking her nose into their training, as always. She really hadn't changed a bit.

By the time we got close, the coach had finished his advice and Austin and Grace attempted the choctaws again. They were still slightly off.

"Grace is coming in late," I heard Mrs Black say as the couple glided back towards their coach, and the coach nodded.

"It needs to be a quarter beat earlier," he agreed, gesturing to Grace and clapping out the rhythm with his hands.

She listened intently, trying to hear her mistake, and against my will, my lips pursed in disagreement, my eyebrows drawing together so much that my glasses slipped a tiny bit down my nose as I looked back to the spot on the ice where they had just completed the sequence, seeing it again in my mind.

Mrs Black and the coach were wrong. Grace had it exactly right. She couldn't fix something that wasn't broken, which made her attempt to correct it a complete waste of time.

"Hey. Magazine girl."

It took me a moment to realize the words were meant for me, and an even longer moment to realize that Austin had spoken them. Looking back, I saw everyone staring at me: Austin, Grace, Mrs Black and the coach.

Paul nudged me when I didn't reply, and I stammered out a single word. "Y-yes?"

"What was that face for?"

~Austin~

As much as I tried to pay attention to Brian as he pointed out Grace's error, I couldn't help but be aware of the woman from the magazine. She and the photographer had crept closer to where we were standing and were obviously listening to our conversation.

When my mom and our coach suggested what the mistake might be in the sequence, the woman pulled a face, as if she didn't agree. As if someone had said something stupid. It almost reminded me of Amy and the way she used to correct our coach when she thought he was wrong, and the memory made me smile. More often than not, she'd been right.

Wondering if this woman could be right too, or at least curious about why she made that face, I called out to her. Since I still couldn't remember her name, I simply called her 'magazine girl'. Not overly respectful, I supposed, but it got the point across. She knew I meant her.

As everyone turned to look at her, she took a deep breath, as though she'd been caught doing something wrong. At that point, I realized I had my hands on my hips, still breathing hard from the dance. Maybe she thought I was mad? With that in mind, I tried to relax my posture to look less threatening and more like I genuinely wanted to hear what she had to say.

It seemed to work since she finally answered me, though she addressed her response to the group in general and not just me. "Grace is perfectly in time. Austin's stepping too early. Just a fraction of a beat."

Grace's lips parted in surprise and my mom's face turned red. "I hardly think that you're qualified..." she started to say, but I ignored her and skated over to the woman, leaning over the boards to try to look her straight in the eye.

"Where's the fraction?"

This close up, I could smell her perfume, a scent I didn't recognize but one which I found rather appealing. Instead of meeting my gaze, she placed her hands on the board in front of me and drummed out the beat of the dance. As her body moved up and down with the rhythm of it, a fact hit me with complete certainty: she wasn't *just* a fan.

She was a dancer too, no question about it.

When she finished, she looked up at me expectantly, but I had been so distracted by her movements that I hadn't been paying close enough attention. "Do it again, please."

She did, and I really did try to focus that time. Even so, I wasn't quite sure I got it.

"One more time?"

Patiently, she ran through the rhythm again and something clicked. I'd been anticipating the step too much and rushing it, just like she said.

"I think I see it."

Returning to Grace, I took her hand and we ran through the sequence a few times, first at half time, then at full speed. When we did it again with the music, it felt better. Our coach nodded at us, and gave the woman from the magazine a nod of acknowledgement as well. My mom, on the other hand, looked furious, giving me a little thrill of satisfaction. She rarely got put in her place so thoroughly, and no matter how much she liked to think so, she was *not* part of the coaching team.

The rest of the session continued without any issues, and before long, the time came to get off the ice. As we exited through the door in the boards, I slid my guards onto my blades and took a towel off the pile, patting my face and neck and slinging it around my neck. The woman from the magazine lurked in my peripheral vision, watching me, but she didn't speak. She seemed to be giving me space, which I appreciated, so I spoke to her first instead. "What was your name again?"

"Mia." With the ice broken, she launched into what she'd obviously been waiting to say. "When you've got a minute, I'd like to have a quick chat about the profile and what works for you for the interviews. I'm happy to work around your schedule."

Since my mom told me I only needed to answer a few questions, I had no idea what she meant, but I would have a better chance of figuring it out if I just talked to Mia directly. "Sure. I'm going to shower and change, and I can meet you in the bar in about fifteen minutes."

"Great, thank you."

The smile she gave me sent warmth spreading through my chest in an unexpected way. Nothing about her was quite what I expected, actually, but not in a bad way. If I were being honest, I found myself looking forward to sitting down with her and seeing what might happen next.

~Amelia~

As Austin walked away to the locker room, I made my way back over to Paul. Mrs Black had claimed his attention again, and she ignored me when I walked over so I ignored her too.

"I'm going to head to the bar. You can meet me there when you're done, or I'll meet you back in the lobby afterwards."

"Sounds good," he agreed, before mouthing 'if I survive' behind Mrs Black's back.

Stifling a grin, I headed out to the lobby and to the club's sports bar. The lunch crowd had just left so most of the tables were empty, and I grabbed one of the comfortable armchairs, hoping to keep things casual for my talk with Austin. We didn't need to get into any questions today; in fact, I would prefer we didn't. All we needed to do that day was make arrangements for me to interview him properly.

As I sat and waited, my mind drifted back to the last time I saw Austin, the day that my whole life changed.

~Four years earlier~

Austin's hand felt cold in mine, even colder than the usual chill inside the arena. I did my best not to look at him, to pretend that everything was normal as we circled the rink, our steps in perfect harmony even though I felt like we were miles apart inside.

"Straight line step sequence," our coach, Karen, called out. We didn't acknowledge her or speak to each other, but we didn't have to. Our bodies were so in tune with each other that as soon as one of us leaned one way, the other followed.

We ran through the sequence four times, each time identical. The steps were perfect, but our coach wasn't happy.

"Get over here," Karen ordered us.

We skated over and Austin dropped my hand as we reached the boards.

"Is one of you going to tell me what's going on?" she asked, looking back and forth between the two of us.

"It's nothing," Austin mumbled.

"If it was nothing, you wouldn't both be looking like robots out there. Now listen: you don't need to tell me what's going on but you need to sort it out between the two of you, immediately. We're going big this year, and we can't afford to waste any more days like today. Is that clear?"

We both nodded mutely. From the corner of my eye, I stole a glance at Austin and took in all the signs of his unhappiness: his clenched jaw, his tight shoulders, the stiffness in his neck. He looked just as tense as I felt.

After our cool down, we left the ice, heading to the locker room together to take our skates off. A couple of other people were in the room, but they both left pretty quickly, leaving me and Austin alone together.

I wished he would just say something. Why was he acting like this? Why was he pushing me away? After what happened the night before, I thought maybe we could finally open up to each other a bit about the tension that had been building between us, but instead, everything felt worse than before.

He *didn't* speak. Instead, he grabbed his bag and headed toward the door as soon as his skates were off.

"Austin," I called out, and he froze. Though he didn't look at me, he turned his head, letting me know he was listening. "You're supposed to drop me off today, remember? My mom's at work."

I got my driver's license the previous month, once I turned sixteen, but I couldn't drive alone yet so I still relied on other people to get me to and from the rink.

Silence filled the air for a long moment before he turned to look at me. His lips were tight, his whole body on edge. "I don't think I can, Amy. Just take a cab. I'll see you tomorrow."

"Wait," I cried out again, leaping to my feet and taking a step towards him. "You heard what Karen said. We need to talk."

"I know," he admitted unhappily. He seemed to be fighting against something with himself, conflicted in a way I'd never seen him before. "I just need to think about some things first, okay? We'll talk tomorrow after the gym."

I didn't want to agree. I wanted to reach out and hold on to him, to keep him there and make him tell me what he was feeling. I wanted to tell him what I felt too.

But I didn't do any of those things. Instead, I nodded and stepped back to pick up my bag from the floor. When I looked up again, he hadn't moved, still looking at me with an expression that I couldn't quite identify. We stared at each other a few seconds longer before he turned and walked out the door.

~Present day~

Austin dropped down into the armchair next to me, pulling me instantly back to the present. He had showered and changed and as his familiar cologne hit my nose, a million other memories swam to the surface of my mind.

Long days at the rink, that masculine aroma drifting around us. When he hugged me at the end of a competition performance, my nose buried against his neck. The way that cologne lingered in the air after he left the locker room on the last day I saw him.

I would have known him anywhere simply from that scent, and he still didn't recognize me at all.

I took a sip from my coffee, trying to drown out the smell of him, and looked up with what I hoped was a professional smile. "Thank you for meeting with me, Mr Black. I get the feeling that you weren't quite as aware of this profile as I had hoped, but I promise I'll try to make it as painless for you as possible."

His eyebrows raised, his head tilting slightly to the side. "What gives you the idea that I wasn't aware of it?"

I couldn't exactly tell him that I'd overheard him earlier, so I left that part out. "I arranged the whole thing with your mother, but you said earlier that she doesn't speak for you. I'm sorry if we should have gone through someone else instead."

He sighed softly, looking away. "No, it's fine. She *does* deal with these kinds of press things. I'm sorry about earlier, I wasn't in a great mood."

His apology seemed like a good sign, and much more like the Austin I remembered, and I gave him an encouraging smile. "It's no problem. We can start over, if you want?"

He returned my smile as he looked back over at me, and my breath caught in my throat. He really was just as gorgeous as ever. "I'd like that. Thanks."

"Okay." I closed my eyes and took a dramatic breath before opening them and holding out my hand. "Hi. I'm Mia Wilson. I'm with Urban Style magazine and we are so excited to be doing a profile on you as one of our upcoming athletes to watch."

Austin's eyes danced with amusement as he shook my offered hand. "Nice to meet you, Mia. I'm Austin. Please don't call me Mr Black. You've got to be close to the same age as me."

"Three years younger," I blurted out before I could stop myself. Surprise pulled his eyebrows up again, and I quickly offered an excuse for knowing that off the top of my head. "I pulled together your basic bio before I came, so I saw your birthday."

He nodded slowly, a smile still playing on the corner of his lips. "What else did you learn about me?"

As he leaned a little closer to me, my eyes widened. Was he *flirting* with me?

He couldn't be. He had never been interested in me like that, and besides, he and Grace were together. I had to be imagining things.

"Mostly things about your career," I said in response to his question. "But I think our readers will be more interested in learning about you on a personal level, about what it's like to train as an elite athlete. That's why I'm hoping we can spend some time together doing the things that you usually do for your training. Hopefully, I can build up a good sense of you as an athlete that way."

Austin leaned back again but his eyes stayed locked on me. "Have you done a lot of these profiles?"

I swallowed as I considered whether I should pretend to be more experienced than I was. The temptation was there, because I wanted him to see me as a professional, but it would be easy enough for him to check up on me if he wanted to. Lying wouldn't be worth it.

"No," I admitted. "This is my first profile like this. But I am a good writer, Mr... I mean, Austin. I sent your mother some of my clippings, I can send them to you too if you want."

Austin laughed, and longing tugged at my chest. God, I missed that laugh.

"I trust you, Mia. What did you have in mind?"

I cleared my throat, fighting to keep my thoughts focused. "I'd like to watch you practice a bit more, of course, but also spend some time with you in the gym, or yoga, or dance class, whatever other kind of training you do."

He smiled again. "You think you can keep up with me?"

That smile and his tone sent a shiver through me. It *definitely* felt like flirting. I'd seen him speak to other girls that way when we were young, when he used to flirt in front of me, thinking of me as a little sister and not someone he might be interested in romantically. Did he behave the same way with Grace, even though they were actually dating? For her sake, I hoped not.

"I can try," I said, trying to keep my voice neutral and professional, but my response only made him smile wider.

"We'll see. I'll be in the gym here tomorrow morning at nine. You can join me, but I'll only talk to you as long as you're on the machine next to me. Once you run out of steam, no more questions."

The challenge couldn't be clearer. Luckily, I knew I was up to it. "Deal," I told him, and his eyes lit up in delight. "I've got to get to class now, but I'll see you in the morning."

I stood up, ready to leave, but his next words stopped me in my tracks.

"I'm heading out too. Do you need a ride?"

For a moment, it felt like all the air had been sucked out of the room.

A ride. If he had given me that ride four years earlier when I asked him to, my whole life might have been different. That decision started a chain of events that altered my entire existence, and now, he casually offered me a ride as if he would do it for anyone, even a girl he just met.

Tears stung my eyes behind my glasses, and Austin frowned as the silence drew out between us. "Mia?"

With all my might, I forced myself to smile, though it must have looked fake. Hopefully, he didn't notice. "No. Thanks for the offer, but I'm okay. I'll see you tomorrow."

I left the bar as quickly as possible, before he could see me cry.

Chapter Four

~**Austin**~

I had no idea what just happened. Mia and I were chatting easily, even flirting a little, and suddenly, she bolted out of the bar like the place was on fire. Reviewing our conversation in my head, I couldn't think of anything that should have caused that reaction, but if it wasn't something I said, why did she run?

The way I wanted her to stay surprised me. Normally, I kept my distance from new people who weren't part of the skating world since I'd learned a long time ago that they usually wanted something from me, but Mia intrigued me.

Obviously, she had a skating background; I knew that from how she helped me with the dance earlier. That made me curious about her, but I also found myself wanting to know what she studied and what she wanted to do with her life and what she liked to do for fun. I wanted to know if she had a boyfriend. Denying it wouldn't do me any good: I found her attractive, and I hadn't even seen what she had hidden beneath that bulky coat of hers yet.

Again, that feeling took me by surprise. I never dated fans, but she wasn't like any fan I had met before.

After a few more moments, I realized I was still sitting by myself at the bar, and giving my head a shake, I headed back to the locker room to grab my training gear to take home and wash that night.

As I passed through the lobby, I caught sight of Mia and the photographer she'd been with earlier signing out at the security desk. They headed towards the door and the guy put his hand on her lower back, sending that same vague twinge of annoyance through me that I felt earlier when Mia smiled at him by the boards. Were they together? I needed to find out before I let myself get too carried away with thinking about her.

The next morning, I got to the gym early, wanting to make sure I arrived before Mia did. It turned out to be a good thing too, since I had just sat down on the mats to start stretching when she walked in. Just like the previous day, she wore her big coat and boots, but as I watched, she finally took them off. The discarded clothing went onto one of the chairs at the side of the room, and she pulled off her sweater and jeans as well, revealing the leggings and cropped tank top she had on underneath.

If I hadn't already suspected she was a dancer, I would have as soon as I saw her in that outfit. She had the long, lean lines of someone in complete control of their body, someone who knew how to use it. As she bent over to slip on a pair of runners, I was treated to a very pleasant view of her backside, and although I didn't mean to stare, I couldn't help it. There wasn't a straight guy in the room who *didn't* take notice.

Standing back up, she finally looked over at me, catching me watching her, and a cute pink blush crept up her cheeks as she walked over.

"Hi," she greeted me, taking a seat on the mat next to me and settling into a few light stretches of her own. Her hair still hung down, covering the sides of her face like a curtain, and she kept her glasses on. Despite barely being able to see her, I still found myself drawn to her. "How did you sleep last night?"

The casualness of the question caught me by surprise and nearly made me laugh. "Is that how you usually start an interview?"

The colour in her cheeks reddened even more. "I know sleep is important for an athlete. I thought it might give me an idea of how ready you are for your training today."

It sounded more like the kind of question a person asked a friend or someone they were close to, but I decided not to push the issue. "I slept fine, thanks. What about you?"

"Same as always." It seemed to amuse her that I turned the question back on her. I caught just a small flash of a smile before she looked down. Her accent sounded a bit stronger that morning than it had the day before, I noticed.

While I continued my warm-up, I also watched her stretch. She had excellent flexibility and a gracefulness in her movements that appeared to be completely ingrained. How long did she skate, and why had I never come across her before?

Those questions lingered in my mind, along with the one about her relationship status, and I decided to satisfy my curiosity on that front first. The easiest way to find out would be to ask her directly. "Is the photographer you were here with yesterday your boyfriend?"

Right when I asked the question, she lowered her chest down to her knees, which meant I couldn't see her reaction. A few long, suspenseful seconds went by before she answered.

"No. Paul works at the magazine, I know him through work. He'll be back to take a few more photos of you sometime this week, once we figure out what works for your schedule."

That answered part of my question, so I decided to press ahead while we were already on the subject. "Do you have a boyfriend, then?"

Her lips tightened, just for a second. "I think you're supposed to be the one answering the questions, not me."

"I'm happy to answer that question. No, I don't have a boyfriend."

Her eyes rolled behind her glasses, and we both laughed. Before I could say anything else, she pivoted into a split and I couldn't keep from staring at her again, my mind going blank as my eyes swept over her limber, lithe body.

All too soon, she pulled her legs back in and brought me crashing back to reality with her next statement. "You have a girlfriend, though. Everyone knows that."

Damn it. She meant Grace. Like everyone else, she probably believed that we were together simply because we didn't deny it. As much as I wanted to tell her the truth, nobody would be happy with me if it got out in this magazine article that Grace and I weren't actually a couple. Painful as it might be, I would have to keep my mouth shut.

Mia seemed to be finished stretching, and I had completed my warm-up too, so I jumped to my feet and offered her my hand. "Come on. Time to work up a sweat."

~**Amelia**~

My hand trembled against my will as I placed it in Austin's, letting him help me up. His touch felt warm and familiar, just like so many other things about him: his lean, muscled body in his workout gear, his teasing smile, the way his hair fell across his forehead when he looked down. Not much had changed, and it made it feel like we'd been hanging out together the week before, not four years earlier.

However, there were also things that *weren't* familiar, things that felt very new. Like the way his eyes moved across me as I stretched, as if he'd never seen my body before, even though he used to be intimately familiar with it. Not in a sexual way, but there probably wasn't an inch of me that he hadn't touched at some point.

At times the day before, I felt my accent start to slip, so I made an effort to play it up that morning, and I also amended my regular stretching routine, not wanting to do anything that might trigger something in his memory. It might be unlikely that he would remember, but I didn't want to take any chances. For the same reason, I kept my hair down, though I would have normally always pulled it back to work out. Through some miracle, I'd fooled him that far, which made it even more important that I get through the rest of our time together without slipping up.

Once we were standing, Austin led me over to the step climbers, getting on one while I climbed on to the one next to him. He punched in a program, and when I copied him, selecting the same one, he gave me a challenging smirk. "You sure you can handle that?"

"Don't worry about me." My response turned his smirk into a wider smile, and I put my recorder down on the machine in front of me before we got started. "You said you'll answer some questions for me while you work out, right? I'm going to turn this on now."

To my surprise, he took hold of my hand to stop me. "Hang on. Everything we've said up until now is off the record?"

Though I didn't know why he would ask, I answered honestly. "Of course. I'll tell you whenever I'm recording or making notes for the article."

"In that case, there's one more thing I want to tell you off the record, before you start. If you can promise you won't tell anyone else."

My heart picked up speed, but whether from the promise of a secret or the feel of his hand still holding mine, I couldn't be sure. "Okay."

The scent of his cologne grew stronger as he leaned closer to me, looking me straight in the eye. "Grace and I aren't dating."

"You aren't?" That genuinely surprised me. Everything I had read and seen over the past couple of years suggested that they were, but when he shook his head firmly, I believed he was telling the truth.

"We let people think we are because the judges like it when there's some kind of real love story with a couple. It's stupid, I know, but our management team all say we should just keep quiet and let everyone assume what they want."

Racking my brain, I thought back to interviews I'd seen with the two of them, and from what I could remember, he was right. They would get asked about being a couple and they would find a way not to answer directly, leaving the possibility open, and everyone else - the media, the fans, the judges - filled in the blanks.

"That must make dating other people a bit tricky," I observed.

He squeezed my hand that he still held in his. "Exactly. That's why I'm telling you."

His meaning couldn't have been clearer, and my stomach twisted. Obviously, I hadn't imagined anything the day before.

Austin Black *was* flirting with me.

The man I dreamed of being with for years was hitting on me, but only because he thought I was someone else. Honestly, I didn't know whether to feel flattered or hurt. Both emotions ran through me at the same time, leaving me feeling off-balance in a way that did nothing to help calm my nerves.

With no idea what to say to that, I simply pulled my hand away. "Let's get started with the workout before my muscles tighten up again. I'm turning the recorder on now."

Disappointment flashed across his face, but it quickly passed and he turned away, pressing start on his machine as I did on mine.

"Let's start with some basic background," I suggested, speaking too quickly as I tried to slow my racing pulse. The accent was harder to maintain if I spoke faster, so I forced myself to slow down. "How did you get started in skating?"

He answered me with a version of the story he'd given in multiple interviews, and that he'd also told me personally, while I tried to pretend I'd never heard it before.

"Like most Canadian kids, I wanted to play hockey when I was young but I couldn't keep up with the other kids. My mom put me in skating lessons to build up my strength. For a while, I did both, but eventually, I found I liked skating better."

"What made you choose dance over singles or pairs skating?"

"My jumps weren't good enough," he said with a self-deprecating smile, which I didn't return because his words weren't true. That was the sound-bite answer. His jumps had been decent for his age but he liked dance better. Why didn't he just say that?

I tried to dig a little deeper. "You must have liked something in ice dance particularly to want to stick with it. What do you like about it?"

He shrugged, but he also gave me a longer answer, one that came closer to the truth. "I like connecting with the music, finding the emotion in it and using my body to express that. And I like how hard it is. Most people think the jumps are harder, but they're wrong. You need to have so much control over your body, over the blade, to make it look like you're not trying very hard at all. But you already know all this since you're a dancer too."

I'd been nodding along until his final words, which sent a spike of adrenaline-laced panic through me. Sweat began to bead on my brow that had nothing to do with the cardio program we were doing.

What did he mean by that? He couldn't have figured out who I was. He would have said something if he had, surely. But if he *didn't* know my identity, where did that comment come from?

"What makes you think I'm a dancer?"

"The way you picked out my mistake yesterday, and the way you moved when you were explaining it. You've done the Rhumba before."

He grinned, looking very pleased with himself, while I breathed a sigh of relief. That made sense, and I supposed it had been a bit of a giveaway. "You got me."

I tried to move on to my next question, but he jumped in before I could. "Did you compete?"

His genuine interest in me was sweet, and flattering, but I would have to be as vague as possible if I wanted to keep my cover intact. "A bit, years ago. Now, when you started competing..."

"Did you ever compete against me?"

He gave me a charming smile, intent on steering the conversation where he wanted it to go, but at least I could answer that question honestly. "No, I never competed against you. Let's talk about this season's..."

"Who was your partner?"

Obviously, he didn't want to let this go, so I pointed at my recorder. "Last time I checked, I was interviewing you, Austin."

With a laugh, he held up his hands in surrender. "Fine, but I have my sources too, Mia. I'll figure you out."

Panic clouded my brain again until I remembered that he wouldn't find anything. He could ask around all he wanted about Mia Wilson. Nobody would know who that was. Nobody in this world knew me by that name.

Still, we were getting dangerously close to the cliff's edge of discovery that I desperately wanted to avoid. Time to take back control of the conversation and get us back to talking about him.

~**Austin**~

Mia shifted the conversation to my training schedule, and although I let her take the lead again, the fact that she seemed so determined not to tell me anything about herself only made me more curious.

Why wouldn't she just tell me who she skated with? What did she have to hide?

It disappointed me that she didn't pick up on my hint about wanting to date her, but in a perverse sort of way, it pleased me too. Maybe Charlie had it right. Maybe I really *did* want someone I could chase, someone who wouldn't fall all over herself as soon as I showed any interest.

Mia wasn't throwing herself at me, that was for sure.

However, she also still hadn't fully answered my question about whether she was seeing someone else. I needed to find a way to bring that up again.

"Tell me about this year's programs," she invited, staying focused on her article while my mind wandered. "What do you like about them?"

She couldn't have asked a tougher question, since I didn't particularly like that year's programs at all. My mom brought in a new choreographer for us since it was an Olympic year, someone who had worked with previous Olympic champions, but I didn't feel like his style worked for Grace and me. Our free dance in particular was very flamboyant and dramatic, in contrast to our usual more understated style. It felt like we were pretending to be something we weren't, and it made the whole thing feel unnatural and forced.

Basically, the programs weren't *us*.

I wanted to tell Mia all of that, but I had to remember that the whole conversation was being recorded and would end up as part of her magazine article. No matter how much I might be tempted to confide in her personally, I couldn't exactly share my concerns with the whole world.

"They still need a bit of work," I answered instead. "We'll be debuting them next weekend at Skate America, so we'll get feedback from the judges and there will probably be changes made at that point."

She opened her mouth as if she wanted to ask something else, but quickly closed it again.

"What is it?"

Mia shook her head. "Nothing. I'll wait until I have a chance to see you working on them later. Maybe we can talk about it again."

The idea of having her on the ice appealed to me, and so did getting her feedback about the programs. Her opinion mattered to me, though why that should be the case, I couldn't really say.

"You've done a lot of great programs over the years," she said next. "Do you have a favourite?"

That question was much easier to answer. Just the thought of it made me smile, albeit in a wistful way. I had never spoken about my favourite program in interviews before and if anyone else asked me, I would have just chosen one of our recent programs for the sake of giving an answer. But since Mia asked, since she made me feel so comfortable and since I knew she understood the basics of dance, I decided to tell her the truth.

"Actually, my favourite is one I never got to perform, one with my previous partner, Amy Gardiner."

Mia's hand slipped off one of the handles of her step climber and she stumbled, taking us both by surprise. She would have fallen off the machine entirely if I hadn't been able to reach over and steady her.

"You okay?" I teased once she regained her balance. Maybe the workout had started to get to her after all, though she hadn't shown any signs of it. "Is this too much for you?"

She wiped her palms on her leggings before grabbing the handles again and resuming her program. "I'm okay." The words sounded a little shaky, but she cleared her throat, and when she spoke again, it sounded stronger. "I, uh... I thought we couldn't talk about your former partners."

Getting back into my rhythm on my own machine, I glanced over at her curiously. "What do you mean?"

"Your off-limit list. 'Previous partners' is one of the topics on there."

"Off-limit list?" That didn't make things any clearer. I didn't even know what the words meant in this context.

Her expression cleared, realization dawning in her eyes, which confused me even more until she explained it. "When your mother agreed to the interview, she sent me a list of things I couldn't ask you about. Those topics were off-limits."

Oh. My jaw clenched as those words sank in, my legs pumping harder into the steps to work off my frustration. My mother really told people that there were things I wasn't willing to talk about, like some kind of diva? I had no idea she did that, and Mia had obviously just figured that out. It embarrassed me both that my mother would do that kind of thing behind my back and that Mia could see it so plainly.

"What else is on this list?"

"I can't remember it all off the top of my head, but I can show you when we're done."

I nodded in agreement. "Please. I want to see it."

We were both silent for a moment, both of us caught off guard by the turn the conversation had taken, but soon, Mia offered me a small smile and tried to pick up where we had left off. "How about your favourite programs with Grace? She's a great dancer."

"She is," I agreed. "I'm lucky to have her as a partner."

Mia's face tightened, catching me by surprise once again. Why would that bother her when she praised Grace first? It brought to mind the way she reacted the day before when I referred to Grace as my partner. Was she jealous of her for some reason?

Maybe that was a good sign for me. Maybe it meant she felt more for me than she let on?

She asked a few more questions, the conversation remaining strictly professional until the program on our machines finished. Only when they stopped moving did I realize that Mia had kept up with me the whole time while simultaneously carrying on a conversation.

"You made it," I acknowledged. Now that I knew she used to compete, maybe it shouldn't have surprised me. She was obviously in great shape. Stepping off the machine, I headed over to the weights next and Mia followed, still holding on to her recorder. I glanced at it in her hand as I took a seat. "Do you think we can stop there for today?"

I only meant that I wanted to stop the interview, not to stop talking to her entirely, but Mia took it the wrong way. "Sure," she agreed, pressing stop on the device. "I'll leave you alone so you can concentrate."

"Wait," I called out as she started to leave. "Can I see that list my mom sent you?"

"Of course. Let me grab it."

Mia walked over to her bag and pulled out her phone, tapping on it as she walked back over to me. When she handed it to me, the email from my mom was already loaded and I scanned through the list quickly, my lips pressing together more tightly with each line.

Complete nonsense, just as I expected. I didn't have any problem with people asking me about anything on that list, and my mom and I were definitely going to have a chat about it.

Did that explain why no one ever asked me about Amy? There had been so many times I wanted to talk about her, to acknowledge or praise her for the influence she had on my skating, but everyone always changed the subject whenever I tried.

Trying to keep the annoyance off my face, I looked back up at Mia, who didn't bear any of the blame for my mother's interference. If anything, I was grateful that she told me about it. "Don't worry about any of this. You can ask me whatever you want. In fact…"

A new idea crossed my mind and looking back down at the phone, I exited her email app and went into her contacts instead. I got a glimpse of a few names, Gaby and Mom among them, before I hit the 'add' button.

"What are you doing?" Concern underpinned her question, but I didn't reply until I had entered my number as a new contact. Showing her the entry, I handed the phone back to her with a smile.

"In case you think of anything you forgot to ask, or if you want to get a hold of me for any *other* reason."

It had to be clear to her what I meant, and Mia swallowed as she took the phone from my hand, staring down at the entry. A few beats of silence passed before she raised her eyes to mine again.

"Actually, I'm hoping to come back tomorrow and see you on the ice again, and Paul, the photographer, could take a few photos of your dance class, if that's okay?"

She might have been determined to stick to business, but I was equally determined not to. "That's fine, on one condition."

"What's the condition?" She sounded suspicious, and for good reason. I was *trying* to put her on the spot, and I grinned back at her as I did.

"You have to bring your skates."

Chapter Five

~**Amelia**~

My fingers refused to keep steady as I did up the laces on my skates the next afternoon, slipping and losing their grip. No matter what excuse I came up with to stay off the ice, Austin insisted he wouldn't answer any questions unless I did, so in the end, I didn't have much choice. Having come that far, I was invested in making the profile as good as it could possibly be.

Why my hands shook was simple enough to explain: it had been a long time since I had skated in front of *anyone* other than Terry, let alone world-class skaters and coaches, and not to mention Austin. No one could blame me for being a little nervous. The last time we skated together, four years earlier almost to the day, replayed in my mind over and over again while I tied my laces, taking care not to use my special knot that might give me away.

Austin sat on the other side of the small changing room, talking and laughing with a couple of the other guys as they all put their skates on. Occasionally, his eyes drifted over to me, taking me by surprise each and every time it happened. In the past, he had always been in the thick of things, the life of the party, while I stayed on the sidelines by myself. Inseparable on the ice but completely separate off of it, the age difference too significant at that young age for us to have much in common other than our career, he never looked at me in the changing room then, no matter how much I wanted him to.

When I finished lacing my boots, I got up and walked out to the rink, leaving Austin and the others behind as I attempted to steady my nerves. The Zamboni still had another round to make, so I went over to where Paul sat in the stands to pass the time.

"Can I take pictures of you out there too?" he asked with a gently teasing smile as he aimed his camera at me, and I smiled back.

"You could, but I'm not going to be doing anything picture-worthy."

I certainly hoped I wouldn't be, anyway. I still had no idea why Austin wanted me on the ice at all. When I asked him, he said it would be easier to explain their new programs with me right there with them, but in my opinion, the view from the boards worked just as well, or better, since I could get the big picture by being a little further away.

Even more than at the gym, it felt strange to have my hair down and my glasses on for going onto the ice. When I skated at Terry's rink, I always took my glasses off and pulled my hair back out of my face, but in front of Austin, I couldn't take any chances. With that thought in mind, I double-checked that my four-leaf clover necklace was still tucked away beneath my shirt. I'd taken it off the day before at the gym, just in case it came loose during the workout, but on the ice, beneath my shirt and coat, it should be safe.

Once the door to the ice opened, Austin still hadn't come out yet, so I stepped onto the ice on my own and made a few laps of the rink along with everyone else, stretching my legs and getting the feel of it. I didn't see Austin get on the ice, but before long, he flew past me, barrelling down the outer edges as he always did. As he passed, he turned and threw me a wink over his shoulder, sending an instant flush through my cheeks.

How could he still have that effect on me? After everything that happened, why did I still react to him as if nothing had changed?

It both frustrated me and, if I were being completely honest, excited me too, with all the excitement a girl with a crush felt any time the object of her affection noticed her. For a moment, blushing under his attention, I felt sixteen again.

After a couple of minutes, Grace joined him and they started stroking together in their joint warm-up. I drifted towards the board to watch them, but Austin quickly pulled Grace over to me.

"You're not standing around watching. Try and keep up. If you can stay in earshot, I'll answer your questions."

I glanced over at Grace to see what she thought of that, but she just gave me an apologetic shrug. Once again, it seemed I had no choice, so as they resumed their warm-up, sculling down the ice hand-in-hand, I followed along behind them, keeping pace but not matching their steps.

Austin did let me ask questions, as he promised. We talked about their on-ice training routines, Grace interjecting whenever she had something to add. Staying behind them as they moved, I noticed Austin had a slight pull on his left outside edge that he'd never had before. Since I knew he had a minor knee injury the year before, it occurred to me it might be related.

When a natural lull came around in the conversation, I decided to ask about it. "Is that pull because of your knee?"

The question stopped him short, and I had to quickly swerve to avoid running straight into him from behind. When I turned and glided back to him, his face had turned completely serious with no hint of his previous teasing or flirting.

"What do you mean? What pull?"

Again, my eyes went to Grace, but she said nothing. Surely she had noticed it? Maybe they just called it something else.

"The top of your edge is tight. The angle's slightly different." I led him back down the ice to where their previous edges were carved and pointed out the difference. "Yours is more angled than Grace's right here. It evens out in the end, so you've obviously adjusted to it. I just wondered if it was because of your knee."

Austin bent down, studying the edge carefully. "I've never noticed that," he admitted before looking over towards the boards and calling the coach over. Together, they examined the edges and the angles while Grace watched silently, her arms crossed.

The longer they spent on it, the more foolish I felt. I hadn't meant to cause such a fuss, and it wasn't like I would include it in my article anyway. My curiosity had simply gotten the better of me.

"I'll have to work on it," Austin said, and I shook my head to myself as I looked down at the edges again. I hadn't realized he could see me, but he must have, since he asked me to explain myself. "What is it, Mia?"

Sure enough, when I looked up, they were all staring at me again, just like the first day when he noticed my reaction. I thought I had a better poker face than that.

Since I had to say something, I stuck with the truth. "If you've been doing it this way for a year, it's become natural for you. You don't want to try and change it right before a competition."

"Better to change it before the first competition than right before the Olympics," he countered, and he had a point, but I still thought I was right.

"It only matters if the judges are going to penalize you for it. If they're not, it's not worth your time. Are you still in physio for your knee?"

He shook his head. "Not for the injury specifically. They told me I had full range of motion back."

I'd heard that before. I'd gone through several therapists who told me there was nothing else they could do for me, until I found someone else who could. "If you want, I can show you some exercises later. I've been through a lot of rehab physio, there might be something that could help."

The offer surprised me as the words came out of my mouth. I certainly hadn't planned to say them, and I wouldn't be seeing him again after the interviews were over anyway. And yet, I wanted him to be as good as he could be, just like I always had.

"Don't do anything without involving Sheila," his coach warned him.

Assuming Sheila must have been the team physio, I nodded. "I'm not a professional, so if you'd rather not..."

"I'd still like to see the exercises," Austin said, cutting me off as he stared at me so intently that I had to lower my gaze, afraid he might have spotted something familiar. Luckily, that didn't seem to be the case since he praised me a moment later. "You've got a really good eye. Nobody else has picked up on that."

Once again, colour rose to my cheeks, but luckily his coach stepped in before he could say anything else.

"Okay, enough standing around. Austin, Grace, we're going to work on the circular step sequence for the rhythm dance first. Miss, could you stand out of the way over there?"

He directed the last part to me, and I quickly moved over to the boards to watch them go through their sequence. As I did, my mind drifted back to a different sequence on a different day, on a different sheet of ice.

~Five years earlier~

"It's still not right," I called over to Karen, who stood next to our choreographer, Mark. "It's pulling us out of the circle."

"It's supposed to." Mark sounded exasperated, as he often did when I questioned his choreography. "That's how you get the difficulty bonus."

"We need to have different holds during the sequence but we don't need to change the hold here. We can keep the Kilian until the end of the next turn and switch after. Keeping the hold will help us keep the direction, no matter what our feet are doing."

"It won't make a difference, and it looks better in the other hold. You just need to run it more."

Mark and I glared at each other for a moment before Austin stepped in, playing the peacemaker as he usually did. "Let's try it Amy's way and see how it feels. If it's not any better, we'll keep working on it as it is. Deal?"

He took my hand and rubbed his thumb across my palm, calming me down as he always could.

"Deal... because I know I'm right," I added under my breath after Mark turned away.

Austin laughed and pulled me down the ice with him. "I'll never understand how you're such a loudmouth on the ice, but as soon as you take your skates off, you go completely silent."

His teasing always made me smile. "They're magic skates, linked to my mouth."

Putting his arm around me, he pulled me close. "We need to find you some magic shoes to wear the rest of the time, then."

We did the sequence again, keeping the Kilian hold as I wanted and as I expected, it felt a million times better.

Looking up at Austin after we finished, I found him smiling down at me as he nodded. "You're right. It's better."

~Present day~

As soon as Austin and Grace finished their circular step sequence, he immediately looked over to me. The way his eyes sought mine, looking for my opinion, made it feel like it could have been that day five years earlier that I'd just been thinking about.

It could have been *any* day that we were on the ice together. It felt just the same to me, and way too easy to fall back into the rhythms of our partnership, but I had to remember that Austin was with Grace, not me, before I let myself get carried away.

Or, even worse, before I gave myself away.

~Austin~

The look on Mia's face as Grace and I finished the step sequence told me everything I needed to know: it needed to be better.

I skated straight over, stopping right in front of her. "There's something wrong with it, isn't there? I can feel it, but I don't know what it is."

"I'm not sure about the rocker in the middle."

Her teeth grabbed hold of her bottom lip as she thought it over, and an odd jolt of recognition passed through me. For a moment, she looked just like Amy, in the way that Amy used to chew her lip when she worked through a problem, worrying the lip back and forth as she reviewed the moves in her head. I hadn't thought about that little habit of hers in ages, but something in the way Mia bit her lip made it spring back into my head clearly.

The conversation we had the day before, about former skating partners and my mom's ridiculous off-limit list, must have brought Amy into my subconscious. I couldn't think of any other reason why I would see a similarity between the two.

Sure, they had the same general build, but so did most dancers. Mia was taller; I remembered exactly where Amy came up to against my body, and Mia had a couple of inches on her in height. Her voice sounded completely different and her hair was a different colour. Their eyes were the same colour, but a lot of people had blue eyes, and Amy hadn't worn glasses.

Overall, they didn't really look anything alike, and I couldn't explain why my brain made the comparison.

"The exit curve is pretty short because it leads into the twizzle," Mia continued, completely unaware of my train of thought as she remained focused on the step sequence I've asked her to review. "If they don't count the rocker because you're not holding the edge long enough, the whole sequence would get downgraded."

The word 'downgraded' brought me back to the topic at hand very quickly. We couldn't afford to give up any points. "But if we extend the curve..."

"You lose the downbeat of the music," she finished for me, using almost the exact words I would have.

Damn, she really did know what she was talking about.

Mia looked past me towards the centre of the ice, seeming to review the steps in her head even though she'd only seen us do it once. "I wonder if you can take the beat from the beginning of the turns. Go into the turns a beat earlier and it might be enough to let you hold the rocker longer."

Trying to see what she saw, I did the turns in my head. "That might work. Let me try."

Leaving her there, I returned Grace and Brian to explain Mia's suggestion. It took a while until I could get the point across, but eventually, we got there. When I glanced back at Mia, her attention had wandered, her feet gliding back and forth in place across the ice as she watched some of the other dancers. It seemed obvious to me that she was itching to join in with the dancing.

Why didn't she skate anymore? What was her story?

"Try it from the top, then," Brian said, pulling my attention back to him and our practice.

While our music got cued up again, Mia turned to watch us, and knowing she was watching made me want to perform well. Ridiculous, I knew, but I couldn't help it.

The first time we ran it, Grace mistimed the changed beginning, so we had to try again. The second time felt better. By the third time, it already felt more natural and flowing than the original ever had.

When I glanced over at Mia for her feedback, she gave me a thumbs-up, and I smiled and nodded back at her in appreciation.

As Grace and I worked through the rest of the program, I lost track of Mia, my attention dedicated to our training. However, when the buzzer sounded to signal the end of the session, I immediately turned to find her, only to see her heading for the open door in the boards.

Not intending to let her go that easily, I sped over in that direction as quickly as I could, blocking the exit with my body. "Not so fast. I haven't seen you dance yet."

Her eyes went wide behind her glasses. "You didn't say anything about dancing. You told me to bring my skates to follow you during your training, and I did."

I hadn't explicitly told her what I wanted, but it had always been my intention to see what she could do. "One dance," I requested, holding my hand out to her. "What's your favourite pattern?"

She looked down at my hand and back up at me, disbelief written across her face. "You want me to dance with *you*?"

"Why not? Pick a pattern dance. I'm sure you know them all. Hurry before they kick us off."

The other skaters had all left the ice, leaving us alone, a fact that she noticed as she looked around. "They'll want to flood," she tried to say, but I wouldn't let her use that as an excuse.

"They won't while we're still out here. The sooner we dance, the sooner we get off."

Her teeth pulled on her lip again, and once more, Amy flashed briefly before my eyes. I shook my head to dislodge the image before offering my hand to Mia more insistently. She did actually have a point that we couldn't take too long or we'd throw the whole schedule off.

"Come on, Mia. One dance. What's the worst that could happen?"

~**Amelia**~

My heart thumped painfully in my chest as Austin stood in front of me, his hand outstretched. This had to be some kind of dream... or maybe a nightmare, I couldn't be wasn't sure which. Either way, he didn't look like he would let me go until I gave in.

Maybe I should just do it and get it over with? As he said, what was the worst that could happen?

He'd danced with Grace for so long, surely he wouldn't even remember what it felt like to skate with me. Besides, pattern dances weren't anything particular to our partnership, they were dances that every dancer knew. I could pick one that we hadn't done very often, one that held no specific memories for us. I didn't even have to skate it particularly well. There was no reason he would have to know who danced beside him.

"Paso Doble," I managed to grit out.

Austin's face broke into a grin and he nodded, calling up to the guy in the sound booth for the music. A small group of the skaters who had just left the ice started to gather back at the boards, curious about what was happening.

He turned back to me, offering his hand one more time. "Okay, Mia, let's see what you've got."

With a deep breath, I placed my hand in his, and the next thing I knew, he pulled me to the centre of the ice.

"I'm not sure how well I remember the dance," I lied. "It's been a long time."

The second part was true. It *had* been a long time, but I still knew the dance fairly well. I still knew them all. They were burned into my brain through hours of study and repetition and I would probably remember them when I was ninety.

"It'll come back to you," he promised.

We reached the starting position and Austin stepped away from me, holding his arms out, my hand still held in his. Trying my best to calm my racing heart, I forced myself to look directly at him. His eyes were full of anticipation and the love of dancing that he'd always had, a look I remembered so well.

Something in that look sparked something within me too. I had been thinking that I could flub the dance a bit, make some mistakes and try to throw him off. But seeing the excitement on his face and remembering how good it used to be, I suddenly changed my mind.

If I was going to do this, I was going to do it right.

The last time I danced with Austin, I hadn't known it would be the last time. This time, I knew. It almost felt like being offered a trip in a time machine, the gift of one last dance with him, and I wanted to make it count.

The music started and without saying anything to each other, we let it go through the rhythm once, feeling the music through our bodies. As it came around to the beginning of the rhythm again, we stepped forward together in perfect sync.

Three strokes forward, and turn. In my head, I said the steps as I did them, focusing on the technical aspect of the dance so I didn't have to think about the feel of his hand in mine. When I turned, his hand wrapped around my back while my hand went to his shoulder, just like it used to. The scent of his cologne hit me once again as I felt his firm muscles beneath my hand, and the last four years fell away.

Our feet moved in unison as we flowed through the steps of the dance, the length of our strokes still perfectly matched. Grace must have adapted to him because he hadn't changed, except he'd become even stronger and more powerful. He pulled me along more than he should have to, doing more of the work for both of us, but that made sense when he was the one who'd spent the past four years training full-time. The chilly air of the rink stung my cheeks as we flew across the ice.

At least I chose a dance where we didn't have to look at each other very much, and I could focus my gaze outward instead as my feet performed all the steps as assuredly as if we'd done this dance together just the other day. I didn't need to look at Austin to anticipate his movement or to know if we were together.

We were. I just felt it.

After four run-throughs of the pattern, I broke the hold and let go of Austin's hand, gliding away from him. The small crowd that had been watching us broke into applause and I nearly jumped at the sound. I had forgotten they were there.

I'd forgotten about everything other than the dance.

Looking over, I could see Grace standing among the others. She clapped too, but her mouth seemed to be set in a straight line, the expression on her face unreadable.

The only person I couldn't bring myself to look at was Austin. Had any of that been as familiar to him as it was to me? Did he notice how right everything about it felt?

And if he hadn't... why not?

~**Austin**~

Circling the ice, my hands on my hips, I struggled to catch my breath. It wasn't just the exertion of the dance that had left me breathless, but how natural and easy it felt to dance with Mia.

It was almost impossible how in sync we were. When I started training with Grace four years ago, it had taken us months to get our strokes synchronized. Even with Amy, although it had been quicker, it hadn't been immediate. How could it happen with Mia without any effort at all?

She was obviously a little out of practice in terms of her strength and conditioning, but her steps were spot-on, the placement of her feet, and the way she anticipated my movements. She had real talent and I didn't understand how I had never come across her before.

More than that, I didn't understand the connection we seemed to have, from the very first moment I met her, and even more strongly on the ice. It overwhelmed me in the best possible way, and it had to mean something. Every minute we spent together, I grew more convinced of it.

My eyes were glued to her, waiting for her to look at me, but she never did. Instead, she headed towards the door to exit the ice. As soon as I realized her plan, I changed course, intercepting her again before she could get there. Snaking my arm around her waist, I pulled her back into the centre of the ice.

"Mia."

I said only her name, waiting for her to look up at me, and when she finally did, the expression on her face caught me by surprise. She looked... nervous, almost, as if she'd done something wrong and I wouldn't be pleased. Hadn't she felt how good that dance was? It felt amazingly good to me, and I decided to tell her so.

"You're very talented. I can't believe you're not still dancing."

As I hoped, her face relaxed with my praise, and she gave a small shrug of her shoulders. "You're a very good partner. I bet you make anyone look good."

She was selling herself short, but I didn't argue since I wanted to talk to her about something else at that moment. The connection we just experienced on the ice had only solidified the way I already felt, and since I probably wouldn't have another chance to speak to her in private that day, I wanted to take advantage of the opportunity while I had it.

"Can I take you out for dinner tonight?"

Behind her glasses, her eyes widened, and I honestly couldn't tell if she looked pleased or not. "You don't know anything about me."

"That's kind of the point. I'd like to get to know you."

Rather than answering me, she glanced over my shoulder to where the doors had opened for the Zamboni to come on the ice. "I think we're holding everything up."

I didn't intend to let her go until she answered. "Say yes, then, and we can get out of the way."

"I don't think it would be appropriate."

Although she gave me a response, it wasn't the one I wanted, and I frowned in confusion. What did she mean by that? Did she have a boyfriend? Why wouldn't she just say so if that were the case?

Sensing my confusion, Mia elaborated. "I'm writing about you, and I'm supposed to stay impartial."

Oh, *that* kind of appropriate. I could work with that. The article would only be a temporary setback.

"So, when the profile is finished, I can take you out?"

"Why don't we talk about it then?" she offered.

"Okay." Although it wasn't a full commitment, at least I had a partial answer. If she would consider going out with me, she must not be seeing anyone else, and I would take that as a win for the time being. Releasing her, I followed her off the ice, my mind already racing.

Somehow, I had to figure out how to use the time we had left together for the profile to convince her I was serious about wanting to get to know her better. My life had been our focus while she remained a complete mystery, but it was a mystery I was determined to solve.

Chapter Six

~**Amelia**~

By the time I stepped off the ice, I'd begun to tremble, partly from the emotions that skating with Austin again stirred up, but even more from the shock of him asking me out. His earlier flirtation had been strange enough, but this extra step threw me completely off-balance.

He wanted to take me out. On a *date*. Everything Amy ever dreamed of, and Mia got it without even trying, without even wanting it. How was that supposed to make me feel?

Paul walked over as I put my skate guards on, taking me by surprise when he appeared in front of me. With everything that had just taken place on the ice, I completely forgot he was even there.

"Mia, that was amazing. You looked as good as anyone out there. I got some great pictures of you guys."

Pictures? Of me and Austin? Panic quickly rose inside me at the thought. "We can't use those for the article."

Even if Austin didn't recognize me, someone else might if they were published.

To my relief, Paul laughed. "Of course not, but I thought you might like to have them. How often do you get to skate with a world medalist?"

Not often enough.

"We should definitely do it again sometime."

Austin's voice cut in from behind me, sending a tingly shiver down my spine. I hadn't realized he was there or could hear us, but when I turned back, he gave me a wink before walking towards the locker room.

"Was he just hitting on you?" Paul asked with a laugh once Austin had wandered out of earshot.

"I don't think so," I lied. Explaining the situation to Paul would be a challenge since I barely understood it myself, so I didn't mention Austin's dinner invitation. "I'm going to go take my skates off and we can grab lunch before the dance class, okay?"

Paul nodded and I hurried away, my mind still racing. There would be time to try to process things later, but for the time being, I simply needed to get myself back under control before I said or did something I shouldn't.

Before I made a mistake that caused Amy's and Mia's worlds to collide.

Luckily, Paul proved a good distraction during lunch and there wasn't any chance for things to get personal during the dance class. With Grace there, along with a few other dancers from the club, Austin didn't say anything further about spending time alone with me. Paul got some good photos of Austin and Grace, I asked a few questions about their off-ice dance training, and we said goodbye for the day.

As he had the first day, Paul gave me a lift back to campus afterwards and on the way, he told me that he had plenty of photos for the profile and didn't think he needed to attend the last interview I had scheduled for the next day.

"We can get together in the office next week to go over them and see which ones you want to use," he suggested.

"That sounds perfect. They're going to be amazing and really lift this story to the next level. I can't wait to see them."

My article had started to come together too. As I reviewed my notes back in my dorm room after Paul dropped me off, I made a note of a few questions I hadn't asked yet that would fill in a couple of the holes in the profile, but overall, I felt positive about the piece.

Austin and I had agreed I would go back the next day for another off-ice workout and one more on-ice training session. That should give me the last few bits of information I needed, and we could both move on with our separate lives afterwards... once I figured out how to turn Austin down if he actually remembered to ask me out again.

Why did he even want to go out with me? I still didn't understand it. He'd never been attracted to me as Amy. Well, other than that one night, which we never talked about.

Which we were *supposed* to have talked about, before everything fell apart.

So, why would he be interested in me as Mia? My body had filled out a bit since I'd stopped training, sure, but that didn't seem like enough to make such a difference. Was it because I refused to tell him anything about myself? Did he just like the fact that I didn't seem interested and he relished the challenge?

And what good did it do to drive myself crazy over this? Whatever his reasons were, it didn't matter. I *couldn't* go out with him. What would I say if he tried to ask me about my past again? What if we started dating and he wanted to meet my parents? At some point, he would figure it out. There couldn't be any future for us.

I might have fooled him for a couple of days but it couldn't go on forever, and once he figured it out, he wouldn't want anything to do with me.

Just like before.

No, the whole thing was impossible. Starting down a road that clearly led to a dead end would be a waste of everyone's time.

Even so, I still didn't know what excuse to give him when I said no, and by the time supper came around, it didn't take long for my friends to notice my distraction.

"How are things going with Austin?" Gaby asked.

"Am I that obvious?" I replied, avoiding the question. All I had told them up to that point was that he hadn't recognized me on the first day, but a lot more had happened since then.

"Obviously in love," Rosa grinned.

We all rolled our eyes at her in unison, but since I could actually use their advice, I decided to confide in them. "It's... weird. He's kind of interested in me."

Three pairs of wide eyes stared back at me.

"Interested in you how?" Jenna asked.

"He asked me out for dinner."

"I knew it!" Rosa crowed, slapping the table in front of her with delight. "He just needed to see what he was missing and he came back around."

"Except he doesn't know it's me," I pointed out. "I mean, he doesn't know I'm Amy. He just thinks I'm Mia."

"But you *are* Mia," Jenna countered. "It's still you, and he likes you."

"Yes, but he doesn't know that Mia is Amy. He doesn't know that I'm both."

"This is making my head hurt," Rosa complained. "Why does it have to be so complicated? Why *did* you change your name anyway?"

Again, all three of them gave me their full attention. Although they all knew about my past, we'd never really talked about why I decided to change my name and register for university with a completely new persona.

"Technically, my name hasn't changed. My full name is Amelia, but I've never gone by that. When I was younger, everyone called me Amy, and now I use Mia instead. It's just a different nickname. It's not that weird."

"But you changed your last name too," Gaby pressed. "Why?"

"My parents got divorced, and my mom went back to her maiden name, so I did too. That's pretty common. Put the two things together, and instead of Amy Gardiner, I'm Mia Wilson."

They didn't look satisfied. "I get *how* you chose the name, but I still don't know *why*," Jenna said.

How could I explain it to them? Most people didn't completely change their identity when they started university, but most people hadn't once been on the verge of being a household name.

"When I stopped skating competitively, I lost a huge part of myself. I didn't know who Amy Gardiner was, if not a skater. Whenever I ran into someone who knew me from that life, they always ended up feeling sorry for me, and I didn't want anyone's pity. I just wanted to move on. So, when I started applying for universities, I decided to use the name Mia Wilson instead. Nobody had any expectations of that name or any idea of what I should be like based on it. A clean slate was exactly what I needed. Does that make sense?"

Compassion replaced the confusion in my friends' eyes. "It makes sense," Gaby confirmed, reaching across the table to squeeze my hand. "And you changed your looks at the same time?"

I nodded. "That's right. New name, new me. I've been Mia for more than two years and it's never caused me any problems, until now."

"So, what are you going to do about Austin?" Rosa asked. It came as no surprise to any of us that she was still stuck on that part of the conversation.

"Well, I can't go out with him unless I tell him who I am, and I'm not doing that."

"And why not, exactly?" Jenna still sounded a little confused about that part. "Why can't he know who you really are?"

"Because he doesn't want anything to do with me," I replied bluntly. "He didn't want to see me then and I'm sure he doesn't want to see me now."

"Maybe he's changed," Rosa suggested. "Maybe he regrets it all. Maybe he's been in love with you the whole time."

"That's a lot of maybes." Despite the ache in my heart, I tried to smile. How many times had I wished those things were true? "For now, I just need to finish this article. One more day with him and we can go back to never seeing each other again."

"And that's what you want?" Gaby's question was soft and supportive, and I nodded, trying to convince myself just as much as them.

"It is. That life, that whole world, isn't mine anymore. I'm Mia now, and my life is here. That's more than enough for me."

~Austin~

Since Mia turned me down for dinner, I didn't have any plans for the evening but I didn't want to be alone either. A strange, unsettled feeling had taken over, as if I stood right on the edge of something big but had no idea what it could be.

To keep my mind occupied, I invited Charlie and a couple of the other guys from the rink over to hang out. We all had training the next day so we wouldn't be doing anything wild. I just wanted the company.

When everyone arrived, we all settled down in front of the hockey game with some healthy snacks, and before long, Rick looked over at me. "Who was that girl you were skating with this afternoon? I haven't seen her around before."

Taking a drink of my sparkling water, I kept my eyes on the TV. "Her name's Mia. She's interviewing me for a magazine article."

"Is that what the kids are calling it these days?" Charlie deadpanned, and the other guys all laughed. Even I cracked a smile, though usually, I tried not to encourage him.

"She's not a skater?" Rick followed up. "She looked damn good to me."

"She looked good to me too," Chris threw in, raising his eyebrows to let us all know he didn't mean her skating ability.

Ignoring Chris' contribution to the conversation, I answered Rick's question. "She used to skate but she doesn't anymore."

"Why not?" Charlie asked.

That was a good question. I had no idea. "I don't know. All I know is that she works at this magazine now."

I actually didn't know much about what she did there either. Looking at the big picture, I hardly knew anything about her at all, so why did it feel like I'd known her for ages? Why did I end up telling her things I wouldn't tell other people, and caring about what she thought of our programs?

"Is she going to be hanging around for a while?" Chris asked next, and I couldn't help but be suspicious about his motivation for asking. As the rink's resident flirt, Chris didn't discriminate between men and women. He tried his luck with me when he first arrived, but thankfully, along with being an incorrigible manwhore, he also took rejection extremely well. It rolled right off him with no harm done. That was part of his charm, and how he got away with hitting on just about everyone who crossed his path and still stayed friends with all of us too.

"She'll be back tomorrow, but that's it." That would be the last time she'd be there interviewing me, at least, but I really hoped it wouldn't be the last time I saw her. Maybe it wouldn't hurt to stake my claim and let these guys know she was off-limits so I added one more thing. "I'm planning to ask her out afterwards."

That got everyone's attention, and Charlie in particular looked surprised. "Does Grace know?"

My teeth gritted together at the implication that I should have to tell her. "It isn't any of her business."

"I don't know if she'd agree with you on that," he laughed.

"Sometimes I'm really glad to be a singles skater," Chris added, shaking his head. "No jealous partner to deal with is definitely a bonus."

That led into some discussion of some of the other pairs and dance couples we trained with and their complicated relationships. I chimed in now and then, relieved the focus had gone off me and Mia, until Rick brought it back around again.

"What about your old partner, Austin? The one before Grace? Did you have the same problem with her?"

The same sense of loss that always accompanied thoughts of Amy tugged at my chest. It had been so long since I'd seen her, and for some reason, when I turned my thoughts to her to answer Rick's question, Mia popped back into my mind.

Why did my brain keep putting the two of them together?

"It was different with Amy. We were younger. She was still just a kid."

That had become my standard answer on the rare occasions the subject came up, and it *should* have been true. At the ages we were when we skated together, the three years between us felt insurmountable, and yet, it didn't change the fact that I had started to think of her differently, to notice her in ways I shouldn't have when she was sixteen and I was an adult at nineteen. Since I knew it wasn't right, I never acted on those feelings.

Except that one time.

Taking a deep breath, my eyes closed against the pain of the memory. Not that night, specifically; that hadn't been the painful part. That moment, so agonizingly brief, had been just as perfect as I'd always imagined. Everything that followed was what hurt to think about, and I didn't need to go down that road again.

It was ironic, really. A three-year age difference wouldn't be a big deal at all at our current ages. Hell, Mia was three years younger than me too. I supposed that meant she and Amy would be the same age, if I had any idea where Amy was or what happened to her.

"When do you plan on telling Grace that you're interested in this other girl?" Rick asked me, pulling my thoughts sharply back to the present.

"Only when I absolutely have to." Getting Grace worked up before Mia even agreed to go out with me would be self-sabotage of the highest degree.

"So, when you're getting married then?" Charlie suggested, making everyone laugh again. That changed the subject to another friend of ours who really would be getting married soon, and Mia didn't come up again for the rest of the night.

Even so, she lingered in my mind long after the conversation moved on. My time with her would be over soon, and I still wanted to get to know her better. Hopefully, the next day would finally give me the chance I needed.

~**Amelia**~

In the morning, Austin texted to tell me that his ice time had been shifted to a later session so he planned to do more weight training and run the indoor track first. He said I could join him for that and for their on-ice session afterwards.

So, wearing my workout gear beneath my clothes and bringing along my skates, just in case, I made my way to the rink for the last time. Just a few more hours and my life would go back to normal.

The new normal, anyway.

When I arrived at the gym, Austin had already started on the weight bench. After removing my outside clothes, I took a few steps in his direction before I realized my four-leaf clover necklace still hung around my neck. Even tucked beneath my shirt, it felt too risky to wear it, so I quickly took it off and tucked it into my jacket pocket before making my way over to him.

Concentrating on his workout, Austin hadn't seen me yet, so I took a moment to admire the way his muscles contracted as he worked. Ever since we met when I was thirteen years old, he'd always been my ideal of what a man should look like, and watching him push himself on the weights, sweat lining his brow and his jaw set in determination, I had to admit that nothing had changed on that front.

If I could design my perfect guy, he would look a hell of a lot like Austin.

Since my thoughts were hardly professional, I shook my head to clear them away and took the last few steps towards him. Finally, he noticed me and flashed me a smile, but didn't stop his reps. I waited patiently for him to finish before saying good morning.

"Hi," he replied, grabbing a towel to pat his forehead and gesturing to the bench next to him. "I've got a few more to do. You want to do some?"

"You just want to beat me at something," I guessed, and he laughed.

"It might help boost my ego a bit," he admitted. "You kept up with me on the steps and on the ice. This is my full-time job, remember? I should be better than you at something."

When I rolled my eyes at the exaggeration, he laughed again. Still, I decided to appease him and sat down on the bench, picked up a couple of dumbbells. "You don't have to worry about my weightlifting. Definitely not my strong suit. But I don't want to distract you with questions while you're working, so I'll keep myself busy until you're done."

We both lifted in silence until he finished his workout, and together, we headed upstairs to the track. He set off at a steady jog and I matched his pace.

"I'm going to turn the recorder back on now, if that's okay?"

"Go ahead."

While we ran, we chatted some more about the season, the future, and what he hoped to accomplish. He wanted to be an Olympic champion, which came as no surprise. What *did* surprise me was when he started talking about what he'd like to do afterwards.

"Skating's not a cheap sport. So many talented kids can't continue because it gets too expensive. I'd love to do something to help those kids keep working on their dreams."

"How would you do that?" I asked curiously, more out of my own interest than for the sake of the article.

"I don't have all the details worked out yet," he admitted. "But it would involve a few different things. Get more kids, especially in the cities, on figure skates at a young age to help pick out the ones who have a natural gift for it. Set up a program where their expenses could be covered by some kind of foundation or donors. I don't know for sure yet. My mom says it's unrealistic, but I think it could work."

It didn't surprise me in the least to hear that Mrs Black wasn't a fan of his idea. She never really cared about anything that didn't directly benefit herself.

However, I thought it had real potential, and I told him so. "I think it could work too. It sounds amazing."

The grateful smile he gave me sent warmth spreading through my whole body. "Thanks. I kind of got the idea from my old partner, the one I skated with before Grace."

The warmth evaporated instantly, replaced by an icy chill. What did he mean he got the idea from me? I never talked about anything like that. Unless he had me confused with someone else? The thought that he remembered so little about me nearly killed me.

Swallowing hard, I tried to sound nonchalant as I asked him to explain. "Did she want to do something like this too?"

He shook his head. "No. At least, not that I know of. I just mean that she kind of inspired it. She was the most amazing skater, so talented and so dedicated. Way better than me, if I'm being honest, and yet, she never got to the level that I'm at now."

Every word out of his mouth confused me more. My situation had nothing to do with not having enough money, so his explanation made no sense to me.

Playing dumb, I pressed him to clarify further. "Did she quit skating because she couldn't afford it anymore?

Austin swallowed, looking down at the track in what I could almost imagine might be sadness. "No, things were different for her. She got injured."

At least he remembered that part.

"But it's what got me thinking about the whole thing. Sometimes, it's just luck that determines whether you succeed or not, and there are kids out there who have the bad luck to not be able to afford to keep going. I can't do anything about Amy's injury, but maybe I can help these other kids. It'd be a way to pay it forward, you know? A way to thank the universe for my own good luck."

I had no idea what to say. Obviously, he'd put a lot of thought into this, and the things he said suggested he did think about me every now and then. So, why the hell did he disappear when I got hurt? Where was he then?

Could I ask him that, as Mia, or would that finally be pushing my luck too far?

Chapter Seven

~**Austin**~

When we started talking about the future, I had no intention of telling Mia about my plans for the foundation. Besides my mom, I hadn't really mentioned it to anyone. It existed only in my head, but as usual, something about Mia made me want to open up and share things with her that no one else knew.

It didn't seem possible that I'd only met her three days earlier. Never before had I felt so comfortable with anyone so quickly.

Knowing that we were almost at the end of the interview process, I'd been trying my best to keep things professional, like she wanted, but after opening up to her yet again, it seemed wrong that I still knew next to nothing about her. Maybe the time had come to change that.

"What about you, Mia? Are you planning to keep working for this magazine when you're done with school, or what's your ultimate goal?"

Her mouth opened for a second and closed again before she answered me, holding up her recorder. "I'm still the one asking questions."

My head fell back as I groaned. "This really isn't fair. I don't know *anything* about you. I'm beginning to think you don't even exist."

She nearly laughed, but before she could, she covered her mouth with her hand. The gesture made me realize I hadn't actually heard her laugh yet, not a real, full laugh, and I wanted to hear what it would sound like.

"You think I'm a ghost?" she asked once she lowered her hand from her face.

That made *me* laugh, even if she refused to. "Maybe. Or a spy? I asked around about you. I asked people who know all the Canadian dancers for the past twenty years and they've never heard of you. One of them suggested you're a Russian in disguise."

All of that was true. After my friends left my house the night before, I went online to some of the skating chat groups and forums that I usually avoided. Reading what people had to say about me had never been my idea of a good time, but those people knew their stuff inside out, and not one of them had heard of a dancer named Mia Wilson. Even the physical description of her that I provided didn't ring any bells for anyone.

It didn't make any sense. She was too good not to have been noticed.

Along with the Russian spy theory, one other suggestion caught my attention, so I asked her about it. "Did you skate under a different name?"

Coming to a stop, she looked down and pressed the stop button on her recorder. "I think I've got enough for now. I'm going to grab a quick shower so I can meet you on the ice later and..."

I didn't let her finish. With frustration simmering inside me, I grabbed her hand and pulled her off the track. I needed an explanation about why she refused to talk about herself, and if that meant being up front and direct about what I wanted, so be it.

Mia took a step back, as if she found our closeness intimidating, but I took an answering step forward, not letting her put any space between us. She kept stepping back and I kept stepping forward until her back hit the wall. When there was nowhere left for her to go, I leaned closer, ready to lay it on the line.

"Mia, I think I've been pretty clear. I want to know you. Since the moment I first saw you, I've wanted to get to know you."

Being so close to her, I couldn't stop myself from reaching out and touching her jaw with my finger. Her smooth skin felt just as soft as I'd imagined, and she swallowed hard at my touch.

That simple motion made me feel a little better. No matter what she pretended, she felt something too. Why was she fighting it so hard?

It seemed the only way to find out was to ask her. "I feel so comfortable with you, like I've known you for years, until I remember that I don't know you at all. For whatever reason, there's a connection here. Don't you feel it too?"

Her eyes met mine again, just for a second before they dropped to my lips, and once again, instinct took over. With my hand still on her jaw, I tilted her head up to me and brushed my lips against hers, very softly. Her breath felt warm against me, her nose pressed gently against mine.

Stopping there, I paused, waiting for her to do... *something*. To say something, or to kiss me properly, anything to show me that she wanted this too.

"Austin, I..."

My heart beat faster as I waited for the next words from her mouth, wanting so badly for her to say she felt the same. I'd never wanted to hear those words so much.

"I need to go."

Before I could react, she ducked beneath my arm and walked away, leaving me blinking after her in stunned silence.

~**Amelia**~

The blood rushing through my ears drowned out all other sounds in the room as I ran away from Austin, heading for the safety of the women's locker room. My heart had never beat so fast before, not even on the ice.

Did that really just happen? Did Austin actually *kiss* me?

Almost?

Kind of.

Not like the only other time his lips had been on me, but a kiss all the same, and with my lips burning from the contact, all I could think of was that *other* kiss on that long-ago night.

The night before everything changed.

~Four years earlier~

Taking a deep breath, I knocked on the front door of a house I'd never been to before, a detached brick building on a quiet, residential Ottawa street. The house belonged to Ben, a new skater who had just joined our club. Not only new to the club but to the city as well, he'd invited a bunch of people over for a casual housewarming party.

When I heard people talking about it in the locker room, I assumed the invitation didn't apply to me. A few years older than me, Ben had quickly fallen in with the older group at the club, the group that included Austin but not me. I never got invited to spend time with them, so when news of the party spread, I expected to be left out yet again.

However, to my surprise, Ben made a special point of asking me if I would come. Actually, he'd made a point of talking to me a few times since he arrived. That kind of attention from a boy was new for me. With all my time spent at the rink and doing my high school lessons by correspondence, I didn't often meet new people, and I had no idea if our interactions meant anything other than Ben being friendly. However, I *did* appreciate the invite, especially since I knew Austin would also be there. Maybe seeing me at a party, dressed in something other than my usual training clothes, would make him finally see me as something other than the little girl that he skated with.

Maybe he would finally realize that I was growing up.

The door opened and Ben's smiling face appeared. "Hey, Amy! I'm glad you could make it, come on in."

Thanking him again for the invite, I stepped past him into the hall. No one else was in sight, but I could hear people laughing and talking down the hall. After taking my coat and complimenting my dress, Ben led me to the kitchen where a small group had gathered.

Instantly, my eyes found Austin. Wearing a grey sweater with dark jeans and holding a drink in his hand, he listened to one of the other guys telling a story, smiling and laughing at whatever was being said, completely oblivious to my arrival.

"Do you want something to drink?" Ben offered, gesturing to a collection of half-open bottles on the kitchen counter.

Although I didn't really know anything about alcohol, I was on a mission to appear older that evening, so I didn't intend to refuse. "What are you drinking?"

He laughed as he glanced down at the deep amber liquid in his glance. "I don't think you want any of this."

My lips pulled down, worried that despite inviting me, Ben saw me as just a little kid too.

My pout only made him laugh harder. "Come on, I'll make you something I think you'll like."

At the counter, he mixed me a drink with vodka and fruit juice, putting a straw in it before handing it to me, chatting the whole time about the things he still needed to buy for his new house. Once we both had a drink in our hands, we turned back to the others in the room.

Finally, Austin glanced over at us and nearly did a double-take when he saw me. The overreaction actually would have been funny if my heart weren't beating quite so fast. His wide eyes moved from me, to Ben, to the drink in my hand, and before I could read his intention, he leapt to his feet and charged over, coming to a stop in front of me.

"What's in that drink?"

I couldn't be sure if he directed the question at me or Ben but I didn't appreciate it either way. What business was it of his? Instead of answering, I took the end of the straw in my mouth and took a long sip of it, keeping my eyes on him the whole time, and his jaw clenched.

Ben laughed again, his laid-back ease a complete contrast to Austin's barely-repressed anger. "Calm down, Black. It's pretty weak. I know you guys are training tomorrow."

"She's sixteen."

"And you never tasted alcohol till you turned nineteen, right?"

Ben smirked as laughter echoed around the room. Until then, I hadn't realized anyone else was listening to our conversation, but it seemed we had everyone's attention.

Austin ignored them all and turned back to me. "Why are you here? Does your mom know where you are?"

God, I hated him acting like I was a child who couldn't do anything on my own. "I'm here because Ben invited me. If you don't like it, you don't have to stay."

"You tell him," Ben chuckled in approval, draping his arm around my shoulder.

Austin shot daggers at him with his eyes. "Can I have a word with you, Miller? Outside?"

A murmur swept amongst the others in the room, everyone anticipating some drama. With a genial shrug, Ben handed me his drink. "I'll be right back."

As soon as Austin and Ben left, all eyes in the room turned to me. With no idea what to say and my cheeks flushing at the awkwardness of the situation, I sat down in the seat that Austin had abandoned and took another sip of my drink. When the others realized I wasn't going to say or do anything interesting, most of them lost interest and went back to their own conversations.

Sitting next to me was Jen, a pairs skater in her early twenties. She'd always been friendly and polite, but we'd never really had a conversation outside the rink. Therefore, it surprised me when she leaned over to me with a knowing smile.

"Is this the first time you've had two guys fighting over you?"

My mouth dropped open before I could stop it. "I don't think that's what's going on..." I started to say, but she cut me off with a laugh.

"I'm just teasing, but Ben likes you, for sure. That's pretty obvious."

Her words brought to mind the way he always smiled at me and the way he came over to talk to me just about every day since he joined the club. Maybe he *did* like me. Huh. That would be a first.

"It's nice to see you here," Jen added. "I didn't think you liked this kind of thing."

I had no idea why she thought that, but I gave her the real reason she didn't see me much. "I don't usually get invited."

A frown crossed her pretty face. "I invited you out for my birthday a couple of weeks ago and you didn't come."

Surprise and confusion furrowed my brow as I stared back at her. "I don't remember you inviting me."

"I didn't ask you directly," she admitted. "But I told Austin to tell you. He said you couldn't make it."

He did what?

A flash of hurt shot through me as I tried to figure out why he would have said that. Did he just not want me hanging out with him and his friends? Was I that embarrassing?

Although I didn't say anything, Jen quickly put things together from the look on my face.

"He didn't tell you? That's not cool. I'm sorry, I didn't mean to make you feel left out."

"It's not your fault."

That much was true, at least, but I had to wonder if this was a regular occurrence? It seemed unlikely it had only been one time. How many times did Austin leave me out on purpose?

As I looked down at my drink, I suddenly had an urge for something a lot stronger, something to try to push down the hurt and betrayal I felt at that moment. Standing back up, I went back to the bottle of vodka that Ben had left on the counter and topped up my drink from it. Ditching the straw, I drank straight from the cup. The liquid burned my throat but I swallowed it anyway, gulping it down until nothing remained.

"Whoa, slow down there." Ben's voice behind me sounded teasing, and I turned to see him standing there with a smile on his face. "You have to be at the rink tomorrow, remember?"

My eyes darted around the room, trying to see if Austin had come back with him. Fuelled by anger and alcohol, I wanted to give him a piece of my mind, but I couldn't see him. "Yeah, I remember. Is everything okay with you and Austin?"

"Nothing for you to worry about. Do you want to see the rest of the house? I can give you a tour."

"Sure," I agreed. Anything to distract from the storm of emotions raging inside me sounded good.

Ben led me out of the kitchen and to the living room where I took a quick look at some of the photos he had around the room. "Where does your family live?"

"They're in Alberta. I've been training in Calgary but I wanted a change, and Ottawa seemed like a good place to go."

He stood close to me as I picked up another photo, this one of him with a pretty blonde girl. "Who's this?"

"That's my best friend, Lily. She's in university in Calgary. She used to skate too, but she's given it up now."

"Wow. I can't imagine quitting."

He laughed, and the sound made me feel warmer. Or maybe it had to do with the alcohol starting to take effect. "I've seen you on the ice and I can't imagine you quitting either. You look like you're made to be out there."

From the corner of my eye, I glanced up to see if he was making fun of me, but he seemed sincere. I placed the photo back on the shelf before moving on to one of him on the ice as a kid, grinning widely. "How old are you here?"

"Seven. That was my first competition. When did you start?"

"At four, but I didn't get serious about dance until I turned ten."

"Such a late bloomer," he teased. "How long have you been skating with Austin?"

My anger bubbled again at the mention of Austin, and I glanced over at the door without meaning to, as if he might be standing there.

Ben laughed again, correctly interpreting my gaze. "He's not spying on you. At least not right now."

My cheeks flushed again, embarrassed that I'd been so obvious. "We've been together for three years."

"So you were thirteen when you started training together?"

I nodded.

"And you guys are going senior this year?"

I nodded again. "I'm really excited about it. You went senior last year, right?"

Although I phrased it as a question, I already knew the answer. Ben competed in his first senior Canadians as a singles skater the previous winter. I always made it a point to know what everyone in the club was doing so I hadn't been checking on him specifically, but he seemed pleased that I knew about it.

"Right. It's tough, but you guys are better than me. You'll have no problem. Anyway, that's the living room. You want to see upstairs?"

He said it casually, as if it were just a continuation of the tour, but the blush on my cheeks deepened. What would be upstairs besides his bedroom?

But so what if he wanted to show me his room? I came there to be treated like an adult and, unlike Austin, Ben was actually doing that. He seemed to like me and there were other people in the house in case I got uncomfortable. I could handle going to his room and seeing what happened rather than running away like a little girl.

I tried to sound equally casual in my response. "Sure, unless you need to get back to your other guests?"

"They've got booze and food, I don't think they'll miss me."

He let me go up the stairs first, following close behind me. The narrow staircase led to an even narrower hallway on the upper floor. As we stood at the top of the stairs, he pointed out the bathroom and a guest room. It seemed really cool to me that he had his own place. Just about everyone else I knew still lived with their parents.

"Who are your guests?" I asked.

"I haven't had any yet, but I'm hoping my family will come visit occasionally. That's my room down there." He pointed to the dark room at the end of the hall, but he didn't move towards it. "Do you want to see it?"

It felt like he was being very respectful, keeping his distance and letting me make the decision. He wanted me to say yes but he wouldn't push it if I didn't. Maybe that made me bolder, or maybe it came back to the alcohol, but I heard myself agreeing.

"Do you have all your medals in there? I want to see them."

Ben laughed as he walked down the hall and flipped the light on in the room, inviting me to follow him. "A few. Not as many as you have."

Considering he lived on his own, the room was neater than I expected. The only other man's room I had to compare it to was Austin's, which I had seen once before, and it had been a disaster.

Ben moved over to a bookshelf that had some of his medals and awards on it, and I eagerly took a look at them, picking up a few to examine them more carefully. He also had programs from a few different events and my eyes landed on the one from that year's Junior Worlds.

"Were you there?" I asked in surprise. He wouldn't have competed since he'd already gone senior, so why did he have the program?

"Not to skate, but yeah, I was there. I saw your free dance. You were amazing, you totally deserved your win."

The compliment made me smile. Personal compliments always made me uncomfortable, feeling like insincere flattery, but when anyone complimented my skating, I believed them. We worked so hard and we *did* deserve to win.

"I actually came to the team mixer at the end, hoping to meet you," he continued, his words taking me by surprise. "Unfortunately, you weren't there."

I didn't know which part of that to respond to first, curious about why he wanted to meet me but also wanting to explain why I hadn't been there. The second part seemed like the easier topic to start with. "My mom's a bit overprotective. She doesn't like me going to events like that."

That couldn't be much more of an understatement. My mom hated the fame that came with my skating and tried her best to keep me out of the spotlight, terrified of people trying to take advantage of me. She didn't allow me to be on any social media channels or even to have an email address to give out to friends. Luckily, she let me have a phone, but only so I could use it in case of an emergency. My parents, my coach and Austin were the only numbers I could keep in it. If I really wanted to, I might have been able to find a way around all her restrictions, but my skating and school work kept me so busy, it didn't seem worth the time or energy to try to deceive her.

Austin had been completely right downstairs when he questioned if my mom knew I went to the party that night. She didn't. I lied to her about getting some extra evening ice time or she never would have agreed that I could go out.

"That's too bad," Ben said mildly. "I'm glad you came tonight, though."

He reached down to take the program from my hands, and his other hand found my cheek, turning my head so I faced him.

"I think you're pretty special, Amy, and I'd really like to get to know you better."

His hand stayed on my cheek, and after putting the program down, his other hand found my waist. My heart began to race from his proximity and the easy, casual way he touched me. As he pulled me closer to him, my gaze fell to his lips, completely subconsciously.

Was I about to have my first kiss? I had no idea how to kiss someone, and I immediately became much more aware of my own lips. They felt a bit dry, but should I lick them before anything happened, or would that be weird?

Before I could make any decision, footsteps pounded on the steps, coming up towards us, and Ben turned to see who was there. His hands stayed where they were, though, and I couldn't seem to look away from his lips even though they no longer faced me.

Lost in my own thoughts, I only realized who had come up the stairs when I heard him speak.

"Amy, it's time for you to go home."

My stomach sank at Austin's tone. He spoke in the clipped, measured way he did only when he got really angry. I'd only ever heard him speak that way to his mom before, never to me.

Forcing myself to look over at him, I saw him standing at the doorway to Ben's room, his face tight and his fists clenching and unclenching.

"It's still pretty early," Ben said calmly, giving my cheek one more stroke before dropping his hand. "We were just coming back down."

"I'm leaving now and I'm dropping her off at her home." Austin's expression indicated he didn't intend to take 'no' for an answer.

"That's not necessary. I can take her when she's ready to go."

Austin's eyes narrowed, making him look even angrier, which I wouldn't have thought possible. "She's ready to go now."

The way they argued about me like I wasn't even there made me uncomfortable, and I decided to step in and defuse the situation. "I can go now." Those words seemed to appease Austin, the tension in his shoulders releasing a tiny bit as I turned back to Ben. "Thank you again for inviting me, and congratulations on your house. It's really nice."

He gave me a warm smile as if Austin couldn't see us. "Maybe you can come back again sometime."

I only had time to open my mouth to reply before Austin walked over and grabbed my hand, pulling me away. "Let go, you'll make me fall," I cried as he pulled me down the stairs, his grip tight and tense.

"Where's your coat?" he demanded, ignoring my protest.

I found it among the pile in the living room and he ushered me outside without giving me a chance to say goodbye to anyone else. His car sat parked right in front of the house and he held the door open for me, as he always did. I dropped into the passenger seat and put my seatbelt on while he rounded the car to the driver's side.

"Are you okay to drive?" I asked Austin as he sat down next to me.

"I wasn't drinking alcohol," he grumbled at me, throwing the car into gear and pulling out onto the street. "We have training tomorrow, remember?"

"Of course I remember. I know the schedule better than you do."

He looked like he wanted to smile at that, but he fought against it. "Apparently one drink is all it takes to make you mouthy?"

I glared at him, which only seemed to amuse him more. "I'm only 'mouthy' because you deserve it."

Any trace of a smile disappeared from his face as he glanced over at me. "What did I do?"

Where did I even start? "You didn't tell me I was invited to Jen's birthday party, for one thing."

A flash of guilt crossed his face, making it clear that he knew exactly what I was talking about. To his credit, he didn't deny it, but he did try to make an excuse. "It wasn't the kind of thing you would enjoy."

"How do you know?"

"I think I know you pretty damn well, Amy."

"You don't know as much as you think you do," I pouted, crossing my arms and looking away from him.

"Well, I have to look after you anyway. Your mom trusts me to take care of you."

My eyes rolled even though he couldn't see it, looking at the road and not at me. "I don't need you to take care of me, Austin. I'm not a little kid."

His jaw set firmly again and that time, he had no response. We were silent for the rest of the drive to my house. As he pulled into the driveway, I had the car door open before he'd even come to a complete stop.

"Amy, wait," he called out as I slammed the door behind me and walked towards the front door.

I spun back to face him, my anger still hot and raw. "What?"

The front porch light of my house illuminated his face as he walked up to me, showing all the conflicted emotions at play there. "You can't go out with Ben."

What on earth gave him the right to tell me who I could go out with? "That has nothing to do with you."

"He's too old for you," he insisted.

"He's hardly ancient. He's the same age as you."

"Exactly," Austin muttered. "And you're sixteen."

"I am *not* a little kid," I repeated, my voice getting louder as my anger grew. Who did he think he was? "I remember you dating when you were sixteen."

"I didn't date nineteen-year-olds," he retorted.

"So I have to date a boy my own age? That would make you happy?"

"No. I just mean..." He trailed off, looking to the side, his jaw clenched again as he struggled to find the words.

"What *do* you mean, Austin?" I demanded. "What does it matter to you who I go out with? Why do you even care?"

When he looked back at me, the conflicted emotions had melted away until all that remained was something that looked a lot like longing. Before I could begin to process that, he suddenly put his hands on my face and pulled me towards him, pressing my lips to his.

I froze.

This couldn't really be happening, could it? It didn't seem possible, and yet I felt his mouth moving against mine and inhaled his familiar cologne, felt the cool October evening air nipping at my ears and heard the sound of Austin's car still running in the driveway. Everything felt vivid and vibrant and far too detailed to be a dream.

Oh, my God. It *was* happening. It was real, and everything I ever wanted.

Leaning into him, I placed my hands on his shoulders as I'd done so many times on the ice, but never like this.

I never wanted that moment to end.

All too soon, when it felt like it had just begun, Austin pulled away. My fingers grabbed at his coat, trying to keep him close to me, but he took hold of my hands and gently removed them from his body. His eyes never left mine, but instead of the longing I'd seen there earlier, a new expression had taken its place.

Regret.

My heart broke open as he stepped back, the regret clear in his eyes, and I nearly whimpered in pain. *Oh, please, no.* Please don't let him regret kissing me, not when it was the best thing that had ever happened to me.

"I'm sorry, Amy." His words were heavy and thick, as if his throat had closed up. "I shouldn't have done that."

"Then why did you?" I whispered. I didn't understand anything at that moment. Why did he kiss me, and why did he say he shouldn't have?

He shook his head, slowly at first, then faster. "I... I don't know. I have to go. I'll see you at the rink tomorrow." Turning sharply, he headed back to his car.

"Austin... please."

I couldn't form any words other than those, but they were enough to stop him for a second. Still facing away from me, his whole body tense, he paused, and I held my breath, willing him to turn back around and talk to me.

He didn't. Instead, he got in the car without looking at me and drove away.

~Present day~

"Whoa, sorry. Hi. It's Mia, right?"

Grace's voice sounded flustered as she backed up, avoiding a collision. I nearly ran straight into her as I entered the locker room, fresh from my kiss with Austin. My cheeks were still flushed, my mind still reeling from the feel of his lips on mine and the intense look in his eyes when he told me he thought we had a connection. I still didn't know how to process that at all.

"I'm sorry, Grace," I apologized, stepping out of the way. "I should slow down."

"It's fine," she said, and I walked past her, thinking she would leave as she'd obviously been on her way out when I came in.

Instead, she stayed by the door, turning to look at me. "You've been here quite a lot this week."

I nodded, trying to calm my still-racing heart and appear somewhat normal. "Yeah. I hope I haven't been in the way too much. I'm coming to your session this afternoon, and that's it. I'll be out of your hair after that."

Although she assured me I hadn't been bothering her, I could see the relief in her eyes when I said that day would be my final one there.

"You used to be a dancer, eh? You and Austin looked good together. It took me ages to match his leg extensions, but yours were spot on."

Rather than calming down, my heart pounded even harder as I tried to figure out where she was going with this. Did she suspect anything about my real identity? "I wasn't really trying to match him, I guess we just have similar technique. You guys look great together. I think this year's going to go really well for you."

I hoped she wouldn't notice that I didn't answer her question about my own dancing, but she brought it up again. "Yeah, I hope so. And what about you? You don't compete anymore?"

I could be honest about that. "No, not for a while now. I'm at university, that takes up most of my time."

"And dating cute photographers?"

It took me a second to realize she was talking about Paul. Why did everyone assume we were dating? "Um, no, we're just colleagues."

That answer didn't seem to please her. "So, you're not in a relationship?"

Everyone's sudden interest in my love life made no sense. Grace hardly knew me. It really wasn't any of her business, so I tried to turn the same line of questioning back around on her. "No. Are you?"

She blinked at me in surprise. "Well, you know, Austin and I..."

She trailed off, leaving me confused. Why would she suggest they were together when he told me they weren't? It took me a moment to understand, but I figured it out: it must have been because of my article. She didn't want me to mention it publicly that they weren't together, so I did my best to reassure her.

"Don't worry. Austin told me you guys aren't dating, but I won't tell anyone else."

Rather than looking relieved, her face paled. "He told you that?"

I nodded, but repeated my promise. "It was off the record. Nobody will hear it from me."

Grace's frown deepened. "But we're not supposed to tell people that unless..."

She trailed off once again.

"Unless what?" I prompted. My anxiety had begun to disappear, replaced with simple curiosity about why we were having this conversation in the first place.

My question seemed to snap her back to herself. "Nothing. Never mind. I've got to grab some lunch before the session, but I guess I'll see you there."

She finally headed out the door and I quickly showered and changed. I still had an hour until Austin and Grace's ice time, but the thought of going out and finding him waiting for me terrified me. Staying in the locker room to work on my article instead felt far safer. Just a couple more hours and I could go back to my new life, leaving Austin behind for good.

Chapter Eight

~**Austin**~

After waiting outside the locker room for ten minutes for Mia to come back out, I had to accept that standing there wouldn't be the best use of my time. Still feeling confused and frustrated, I went back to finish my run, had a shower and got changed before heading back to the rink. At least she would be joining me on the ice again, but that was the last session we had scheduled and I still had to find a way to convince her to go out with me once we were finished.

Her behaviour had me stumped. Why did she run away? Why wouldn't she just admit that she felt something too, since I felt certain she did? In the locker room, the guys joked around as usual while we got our skates on, but my mind lingered on the mysterious woman who'd rarely left my thoughts since I met her. Hopefully, I hadn't completely scared her off, but I had no idea how to win her over in the limited time we had left.

When I walked out to the arena, my eyes found her immediately, sitting in the stands, watching the Zamboni on the ice, and I headed straight over to her.

"I thought you might bail on me," I told her, glancing down at her feet which were still in her boots. "Where are your skates?"

Her smile looked more nervous than ever. "I don't want to be in the way. I can watch you from here and ask any last questions I have afterwards."

That wouldn't work for me. I needed as much time with her as possible, and that meant being on the ice together. "Do you have your skates with you?"

"Yes, but I don't need to…"

"Go put them on," I instructed. "I want your opinion on something in our free dance."

Although that was true, she could give her opinion just as easily from the boards, so I quickly made my way onto the ice before she could point that out. Thankfully, my plan worked. By the time Mia got her skates on, Grace and I were already working on the lift that I wanted Mia to take a look at. She stayed near the boards as she came onto the ice, watching us carefully.

Grace and I ran the lift one more time before returning to the boards where our coach and choreographer waited. I caught Mia's eye and gestured for her to come and join us.

"How bad is it?" I asked as she skated up to us.

"How bad does it feel?"

The response, so blunt and to the point, made me laugh. It almost sounded like something Amy would have said.

"When we're in position, it's not bad."

I left it there, curious to see if Mia had spotted the problem I had with it, and of course she had. "It's just that the entry is wrong."

"Who is this?" our choreographer asked, giving Mia a wary once-over as she criticized his lift. He might not like her bluntness, but his feelings weren't my top priority. I just wanted to fix the lift.

"Someone who knows what she's talking about," I told him before turning back to Mia. "What would you suggest?"

Rather than replying directly to me, she looked over at Grace. "What do you think? How does it feel for you?"

Grace's eyebrows raised, looking surprised to be included in the conversation. To be fair, no one normally asked her what she thought about our programs.

"I... I think it's okay," she said, glancing at the choreographer whose patience seemed to be wearing thinner by the second. "We just need to practice it more."

In some situations, that might have been true. Some things were hard and needed practice, but others just didn't feel right, and this lift fell into the latter category.

Mia clearly didn't agree either, but she tried to keep a conciliatory tone. "Maybe try it this way instead, just to see if it's better or not."

Her small, soft hands directed mine, placing them where she wanted them to go on Grace's body as she ran us through a modified entry. Once Grace and I both thought we had it, we ran through it in slow motion a few times.

"Are you ready to give it a shot?" I asked Grace.

Still looking uncertain, she nodded. With me whispering encouragement to her, we ran the entry a couple of times at full speed before trying the full lift with the new entry.

It was better.

So much better.

I could hardly believe how good Mia's eye was and how quickly she picked up on what would work for us. I *needed* to know more about her.

Still holding Grace's hand, I skated back over to Mia. "That's perfect. It's the same level of difficulty, but feels much more natural."

Mia turned to my partner again, determined to involve her in the process. "How was it for you, Grace?"

Grace's response was less enthusiastic, but still in agreement. "It feels smoother."

When I looked over at Brian, he nodded his head in acceptance. "We'll change it."

The choreographer wouldn't be happy, but Brian could deal with that. Getting the dance right was much more important.

As we moved on to some of the other elements of the free dance, Mia followed behind us with her recorder, asking questions about the dance and our hopes for the season. Staying entirely focused on our skating, she left me no opportunity to make things more personal. Not that I could have really done so anyway with Grace right beside me the whole time.

Finally, the session came to an end and Mia switched her recorder off. The little clicking sound made my heart beat faster. If she had finished the interview, I could ask her out again. I'd been waiting all day for that moment, but I still didn't know the best way to do it.

She seemed to respond well when I challenged her to keep up with me on my workouts. Her competitive side shone through in that scenario, so maybe I could make my dinner invitation a competition too?

My eyes fell on the recorder in her hand, and in a split second, I made my decision, reaching over and snatching it away from her.

"Hey!" she protested. "Careful with that."

With a smile, I skated backwards away from her, holding the recorder out in front of me. "You can have it back if you agree to go out for a drink with me tonight."

"I already told you..." she tried to protest as she skated towards me, but I shook my head.

"You said you couldn't go out with me while interviewing me, but we're done now, right? You've got everything you need, so there's nothing stopping you now."

Pursing her lips, she made a grab for the recorder. I managed to dodge her at the last second, laughing.

"You think you can catch me?"

"I *know* I can catch you. I just don't want you dropping my recorder."

A smile had started to tease the corner of her lips and I grinned back at her, loving her competitive spark.

"Austin, come on," Grace called from the boards. "They're waiting to flood."

I ignored her, all my attention focused on Mia. "How about this? I'll give you one minute to catch me. If you do, you can have the recorder back."

"Fine," she agreed, and my eyebrows raised.

"Wait, don't you want to know what happens if you don't catch me?"

Mia shook her head. "It's not going to happen, so it doesn't matter."

Her confidence was admirable, despite being misplaced. "Well, I'll tell you anyway. If you don't catch me, you'll go out with me tonight and I'll give the recorder back to you then."

~**Amelia**~

Once Austin laid out the conditions of his challenge and I agreed, he called out for someone to start timing us. For a moment, we both stood still, each waiting for the other to make the first move, and my brow furrowed. Why didn't he try to get away?

Belatedly, I realized he must have been trying to wind the time down, so I would need to move first. Sprinting from my position, I took off towards him, my blades digging into the ice to propel me forward.

He dodged me easily, his delighted grin making my stomach flip the same way it always had.

In theory, he had the advantage. Thanks to his full-time training, my speed couldn't begin to match his. However, there was one important thing he hadn't taken into consideration.

We'd played this game before.

~Five years earlier~

"Hey!" I called out in indignation as Austin snatched my journal from my hands. "Give that back!"

He smirked, his eyebrows raising in a playful tease. "You want it? Come and get it."

Turning his back to me, he took off down the ice while I struggled to control my panic. If he turned the book open to the last page where I had just been writing, he would only find my thoughts and ideas about our dance. That would be no big deal.

But if he happened to look at some of the *other* pages, the ones where I talked about the way he made me feel…

No. I refused to even imagine that happening, the thought far too mortifying to entertain. No matter what, I had to get it back before he saw anything.

Throwing my pen down on the boards, I took off after him, trying to cut him off as he rounded the corner but he easily dodged me and doubled back the way he came.

"What do you write in here anyway?"

He began to flip through the pages while skating, making my heart pound far harder than the exertion of chasing him did.

"It's private. Give it to me!"

He made no move to obey me. Instead, he paused on a particular page, reading something that made his brow furrow.

No! What was he looking at? The adrenaline that shot through my body, along with his distraction as he squinted at the page, gave me the edge, and I managed to grab the book from his hands, quickly lifting my shirt and shoving it underneath. He wouldn't dare to take it from there.

"Amy, wait," he called out as I hopped off the ice, heading to the locker room without even stopping for my guards. Feeling like my lungs were closed off, I gulped in air, trying to calm the terror churning in my stomach. What had he seen? How could I ever face him again if he knew how much I thought about him?

Austin entered the locker room just after I flung myself onto a bench and sat down next to me. "Hey. Don't be mad."

"I told you it's private," I whispered, reaching down and untying my laces so I wouldn't have to look at him. My cheeks must have been flushed a deep red since I could feel them burning.

"Well, maybe it shouldn't be."

Despite myself, I looked up at him, my shock overriding my embarrassment. "What?"

He couldn't actually mean that he wanted me to tell him how I felt, could he?

For just a moment, wild hope bloomed in my chest and I could see it playing out in front of my eyes, just like I'd always imagined: he'd tell me he felt the same, that he always had, and he'd ask me to be his partner off the ice too. It felt so close that I could almost reach out and touch it.

Just as quickly, his next words brought my hopes crashing back down again.

"You've got some good ideas in there. It looked like a new lift?"

Oh. He found one of the pages about skating. Of course that was what he meant about not keeping things private. It had nothing to do with him at all, which should have been a relief. I didn't want him to know how I felt.

Did I?

"I, uh, I just write down some things I think would look good," I said as my panic slowly receded, replaced by a dull ache of disappointment. "I don't know if we could even do half of them."

"We should try them," he encouraged me. "You've always got such good ideas about our programs. You could probably create one all by yourself."

With one last encouraging smile, he stood up and went over to his locker on the other side of the room as a couple of his friends drifted in and he turned his attention to them.

His words echoed in my head as I finished changing. I'd dreamed about creating my own program, but I didn't think anyone would actually let me. No one choreographed their own programs at fifteen.

But if Austin backed me up, maybe I could try.

Maybe nothing was as impossible as it seemed.

~Present day~

Austin skated just in front of me as I chased after him, his back to me, which gave me the perfect angle. All I had to do was look for his telltale signals, subtle shifts in his body that would tell me which direction he intended to go, whether he realized it or not. Sure enough, the muscles in his left leg tightened, giving me plenty of warning. Although he twisted his upper body to the left to try to throw me off, I was ready for him.

When I turned right, he almost ran straight into me as he tried to double back away from me. As he stumbled to avoid hitting me, I grabbed the recorder from his hand.

"Got it," I exclaimed in triumph, and disappointment flashed across Austin's face.

It didn't last long, though, replaced almost immediately by determination. "Not if I get it back before the time runs out."

"That wasn't part of the deal," I protested, quickening my pace to try to keep ahead of him but it did me no good. He caught up to me easily, his arms snaking around my waist to stop me from slipping away.

Seeing no other alternative, I dropped the recorder down my shirt, into my bra. That should have been the end of it. It certainly stopped him the last time.

But this time, he leaned over my shoulder, his face against mine as he whispered in my ear. "If you think that's going to scare me off, you're badly mistaken."

A flash of heat ran through my whole body at the idea of his hand down my shirt and I tried to pull away, but his strong arms didn't loosen their grip at all. I must have looked like one of those cartoon characters, my legs pumping but my body staying resolutely in one place.

"Everyone's watching," I reminded him. To my chagrin, my voice shook slightly, but my words were still true. A small group had gathered along with the Zamboni driver waiting for us to get off the ice.

Austin didn't pay them any attention, his voice still low and sexy in my ear. "Tell me, Mia: are you ticklish?"

Oh, no. I squirmed again, trying to get loose, as his fingers started to poke at my ribs. "Austin, don't..." I pleaded, but he didn't budge. His fingers pressed down and I wriggled helplessly, starting to laugh.

"I'll stop if you give it back," he bargained, his hand reaching into my jacket pocket to get even closer to my ribs with one less layer of fabric in the way.

I pulled away from him as hard as I could just as he pressed down harder, and the pressure made me laugh harder.

So hard that I snorted. *Loudly.*

Immediately, my hands covered my mouth as my stomach dropped. *Oh, God.* He must have heard that. All week, I'd done my best not to laugh in front of him in case I snorted just like that. He hadn't recognized my voice or my face since I'd done my best to disguise them, but I couldn't hide my laugh.

My heart in my throat, I turned back to look at him, but to my surprise, his eyes weren't on me. Instead, he stared down at his hand, his jaw hanging slack.

When I looked down too, my stomach bottomed out completely.

His hand must have come out of my pocket when I pulled away from him, taking with it the necklace I had shoved in there earlier. The four-leaf clover sat in his hand, the bright green enamel shining under the lights of the rink.

The four-leaf clover he gave me on the day of our first competition together.

"Black!" A voice called out from behind us, from someone wanting us to get off the ice, no doubt, but I felt frozen to the spot, and Austin hadn't moved either. He continued to stare at his hand, looking at the necklace as if it held the answers to life's deepest mysteries.

Finally, he raised his eyes to mine, and I couldn't deny the truth I saw there. *He knew*.

"Amy?" he whispered.

Chapter Nine

~**Austin**~

The whole world narrowed around me until I couldn't see anything other than the four-leaf clover in my hand. No sound existed except for Mia's snorted laugh echoing in my ear.

No, not Mia's.

Amy's.

Even though I hadn't heard that laugh for four years, I never forgot it. For months after she disappeared, every time I heard anyone snort through their laughter, hope swelled within me, hoping that it would be her and that she'd come back to me.

That she'd forgiven me.

Invariably, the sound came from someone else, never her, and the loss would hit me all over again, followed by the guilt that never fully went away.

Eventually, I stopped hoping. It was easier that way.

Hearing that laugh out of Mia's mouth, I might have still refused to make the connection. I might have thought that she sounded a little like Amy, just as so many other little things over the past few days had reminded me of Amy. I would have chalked it up to another coincidence and left it at that.

The necklace, however, I couldn't explain away. Dozens of memories flashed through my mind as I stared at it. Sitting at my computer, searching through websites before placing a custom order for a chain that wouldn't break while we skated. The sweet smile on her face when I gave it to her before our first competition. Seeing it sparkling beneath the arena lights and camera flashes when we won the Junior World Championships.

The necklace *couldn't* be a coincidence, and it could only mean one thing: the girl in front of me, the one I'd just spent four days with and felt a connection with right from the beginning, wasn't a stranger to me at all.

"Amy?"

The word came out of my mouth in a whisper as I looked into her eyes. *Her* eyes. How did I truly not realize until that moment that, beneath the glasses, those were Amy's eyes looking at me?

It seemed impossible, now that I knew, but an even bigger question rose behind it: why on earth did she hide from me? Why did she pretend to be someone else?

What the hell was going on?

Before I could ask any of those questions, before I could say anything at all, Amy grabbed the necklace from my hand and darted away, heading for the exit.

"Austin!" Brian yelled from the boards. From his tone, it sounded like he'd been trying to get my attention for a while. My thoughts still flying in a million directions at once, I turned to him. "Get off the ice! You're holding everyone up."

Seeing that Amy had almost reached the door already, my body finally reacted and I took off after her. By the time I stepped off the ice and grabbed my guards, she already had hers on. Rather than looking back at me, or saying anything at all, she headed to the stands where she'd left her bag, picked it up and kept going, heading towards the main door that led to the club's lobby.

Where was she going? She still had her skates on. She couldn't just leave.

And yet, she did. Pushing the door open, she headed out to the lobby. Seeing her disappear through the door finally roused me from my stupor and, still in my skates myself, with Grace calling after me, I followed.

When I pushed the door open, no more than thirty seconds after she'd gone through it, Amy was nowhere to be seen.

Looking back and forth, my eyes scanning every corner, frustration coursed through my veins. She couldn't just disappear again. Why had she come at all? Had this been some kind of game to her, to see how long it would take me to realize who she was?

What did any of this mean?

Grace came up behind me as I stood uselessly in the lobby, water dripping from my blades and forming a small pool at my feet. "Austin? What's going on?"

I wished someone would tell me, because I had absolutely no idea.

"It's nothing," I muttered before turning back to head to the locker room. Grace was the last person I could talk to about this. The only one who could help me understand was Amy herself, and she just vanished.

Just like before.

As quickly as possible, I got changed, threw my clothes in my bag and headed home. I needed to go somewhere quiet and think, to try to figure out what was going on and what to do next.

The present and the future should have been my focus, but no matter how hard I tried to avoid it, my mind kept pulling me back to the past.

~Four years earlier~

I made such a mess of everything.

That solitary thought kept running through my head as I drove home from the rink after practice. I didn't want to leave Amy without a ride home but having the conversation we needed to have felt impossible. I still had no idea how to explain to her why I kissed her the night before and why it couldn't happen again.

It had been a stupid, stupid thing to do.

Nothing could happen between us, at least not yet. I'd been telling myself the same thing, over and over, for the last year.

I couldn't pinpoint exactly when my feelings for her started. I didn't wake up one day and decide, 'hey, I like Amy now.' No, instead of a big moment of realization, it had been a lot of little things, building up slowly over time.

One day, putting my hands on her inner thighs for a lift, like I'd done a million times, suddenly felt more intimate than it ever had before. I started to find it cute when she pinched the top of her nose to try to stop herself from snorting when she found something funny. And even though I dated a pretty steady stream of girls, at the end of each day, I found myself wanting to talk to Amy instead.

The timing couldn't have been worse. Having just turned eighteen, I was legally an adult while she remained very much a teenager. Legality aside, the idea of dating a fifteen-year-old didn't appeal to me in general, but Amy was different. Mature for her age, she was my partner and my friend, and the girl who knew me better than I knew myself sometimes.

And the girl whose very protective mother made me promise that I would keep her safe and that I wouldn't let anyone try to take advantage of her.

Knowing how much Amy's mom worried about her, I assured her that I would always look out for her. That was the reason I didn't pass on invites like the one to Jen's birthday, since Amy's mom would never agree to let her go and I didn't want Amy to be disappointed or frustrated when her mom refused. It seemed better to me that she never knew she'd been invited.

It took a long time, but her mom finally trusted me enough to be alone with Amy on the drive to and from the rink. If she knew the way I really felt, she would put an end to it immediately. I didn't want to betray her mom's trust and I didn't want to lose that time with Amy either.

So, I forced myself to keep my distance. I flirted with other girls, dating them occasionally, but I never got seriously involved with anyone. How could I, when I already knew exactly who I wanted to be in a relationship with?

As the year went on and we both turned another year older, things got even harder.

Amy got a little taller, a little more developed. We had to relearn some of our basic techniques to adjust for the changes to her body, and we had no choice but to be comfortable with touching each other. That had always been part of the job, but it didn't stop my body from reacting if I accidentally touched her or she accidentally touched me in places that we hadn't meant to.

As if all of that wasn't enough to drive me insane, other skaters at the club started paying attention to her, and the idea of her dating any of them made me feel slightly sick. I remembered very well what I'd been like at sixteen and I didn't want any of those horny little bastards going anywhere near her.

Yet somehow, despite all of the tension, I'd been handling it. I'd been keeping myself in check, not letting anything slip.

Until Ben showed up.

At nineteen, he was the same age as me. A couple of months older, in fact, but that didn't stop him from showing an interest in Amy. When he invited her to his house and gave her a drink... I couldn't take it. I just couldn't.

If I couldn't have her, then he couldn't either.

"You need to back off," I snapped at him as soon as we were outside his house. Despite the chill in the air, the anger boiling inside me stopped me from feeling the cold. "If you want to be friends with Amy, that's fine, but anything else is off-limits."

He laughed at me. He actually laughed. "I don't think that's your decision. She's capable of making up her own mind."

My jaw tightened as he twisted my words. I would never suggest Amy couldn't make her own decisions, but this went deeper than that. "She's sixteen years old," I repeated, echoing what I told him in the kitchen when he mixed her a drink. "And you're an adult."

I'd told myself the same thing in the mirror more times than I could count.

Ben's eyebrows lifted in a way that felt almost more condescending than his laughter. "I'm not sure exactly what you think I have in mind. I'm not looking for a hook-up. I just want to get to know her better."

I had tried to tell myself that too: there wouldn't be anything wrong with us just dating. We didn't have to sleep together. However, I knew how it would look. I had to think about her reputation, and *our* reputation too, as athletes. If word got around that we were together, the rumours would be rampant, and it could affect the way the judges viewed us too.

Putting our career in jeopardy was the one thing I absolutely wouldn't do, not when I knew just how much it meant to her.

"Well, she's too busy for dating right now. She's completely dedicated to our training, and her mom would never allow it anyway."

Those things were all true too. It wasn't hard for me to think of reasons not to date Amy, since I'd been doing it for the past year.

Ben gave me a cool, appraising look. "In that case, I'm sure she can tell me that herself. If anyone needs to back off here, it's you. You're not her father, her brother or her boyfriend, so I don't see how you have any say in what she does at all. Now, you can stay out here if you want, but I've got a party that I'm supposed to be hosting."

He turned and went back into the house while I clenched my fists tighter, resisting the urge to scream into the night air. This was completely unfair. If she actually went out with him, I didn't know how I could handle it. The idea of anyone other than me being her first boyfriend made me want to punch a hole in the wall.

I had to get her out of there and give myself a chance to calm down so I could speak to her about this with a cool head.

Jogging to my car parked further down the street, I got in and drove up to stop right in front of the driveway. With the getaway secured, I headed back into the house, looking for her. She'd left the kitchen and Ben was nowhere in sight either. I asked the others where they went, but no one knew.

My stomach sinking, I moved through the other rooms downstairs before looking up the stairs. *If he took her up to his room...*

My mind went completely blank as I raced up the stairs and to the door of the bedroom, stopping short at the sight that greeted me there. His hands touching her were like a punch to my gut, and I knew I sounded crazy when I forced her to leave with me. Obviously, she thought I'd lost my mind.

I meant to drop her off and leave, giving us both time to cool down, but I didn't.

I kissed her instead.

If she'd pushed me away or slapped me or done anything to show that my kiss was unwelcome, that would have made it easier.

Instead, she kissed me back sweetly, and it exceeded every expectation I had. Her lips were made for mine. I'd never felt anything like it before and for one brief, wonderful moment, I let myself enjoy it.

All too soon, reality crashed back down around me. All the reasons why it couldn't happen and why I shouldn't have done it raced back into my head, and filled with guilt and confusion, I left before I could make things worse.

At practice earlier that day, she barely looked at me. From the tension in her body, I knew that she was hurting, and probably very confused, but I didn't know how to make it right. We needed to find a way to move past it, but first, I had to figure out exactly what I wanted to say.

For that, I needed time alone to think, and I refused to drive her home to try to give myself that time.

The next time I saw her, I would have it all figured out, and I would finally tell her the truth.

~Amelia~
~Present day~

As soon as I made it through the door of the practice rink, I broke into a run. All I could think about was getting out of there before Austin followed me and I had to explain myself to him.

How could I have been so stupid? I let my guard down, got too close, and now he knew. He knew it was me and he knew I lied to him.

What would he do? Would he say something to the magazine? Maybe I hadn't technically misrepresented myself, but there were definitely grey areas around the edges. I could lose my internship over this, and possibly get in trouble with the university too. And those weren't even the things that worried me the most.

No, the worst part had been the look on his face when he looked up at me, the hurt and confusion in his eyes, as if *I'd* betrayed *him*.

Tears gathered in the corners of my eyes, but I blinked them back furiously. How dare he look at me like that after everything that happened? He left *me* behind, not the other way around. If anyone had a right to be bitter and hurt, it should have been me.

When I finally got away from the rink, through the parking lot and out to the sidewalk, I sat down on the curb and untied my skates, pulling them off and changing into my boots right there on the pavement. Anybody passing by probably thought I was crazy, but I didn't care. My hands shook so badly that I could barely shove my skates back into my bag as my memories pulled me back to the day that changed my life forever.

~Four years earlier~

Bright lights. Painfully bright.

They were the first thing I noticed as I tried to open my eyes, and I pressed my eyelids tighter together instead, hoping that would bring me some relief. It didn't make much of a difference. My eyes hurt, my head hurt and my back hurt. In fact, pretty much everything hurt.

Where was I? What was going on?

"Amy? Honey?" My mom's voice sounded different somehow. Raw. Hoarse.

"Mom?" I tried to reply, but the word came out more like a croak.

"She's awake," I heard her say, her voice still sounding strange as she spoke to someone I couldn't see. A moment later, a gentle hand caressed my cheek and my mother spoke again, closer to me. "It's okay, sweetheart. You're going to be okay."

I didn't feel that way, but I also had no idea what happened to me. "What's going on?"

My throat scratched and my lips were parched. My discomfort must have been obvious because a moment later, someone placed a straw in my mouth. Gratefully, I took in the cool water, but my relief only lasted a moment before I started to choke on it. My mother swore as I coughed, pain shooting through my body with each movement.

When the coughing stopped, I finally managed to open my eyes enough to see the bright, white room around me. Overhead panel lighting and the steady beep of machines told me it must be a hospital, and the arrival of two nurses a moment later seemed to confirm it.

"Hi, Amy," one of them said to me with a bright smile. "It's great to finally meet you. I'm Angie and this is Laura. We're going to ask you a few questions to see how your head's doing."

"My head hurts," I told her preemptively, and her lips pursed in sympathy.

I'm sure it does, but the fact that you answered me so quickly is a really good sign. Do you remember your name and how old you are?"

Was she serious? I glanced at my mom, unsure how I should respond, but the tightness around her mouth and her red-rimmed eyes suggested no one was joking, so I answered earnestly. "I'm Amy Gardiner and I'm sixteen."

Angie nodded as she checked some of the numbers on the machine next to me. "Perfect. And can you tell me something else about yourself?"

"I'm a figure skater."

It was the first thing that popped into my head, but as soon as the words were out, my mom covered her mouth with her hand and the two nurses exchanged concerned glances. What did that mean? Surely that wasn't the wrong answer?

"What's the last thing you remember?" Angie asked next.

I hadn't thought about that yet, so I took a moment to try to reach back into my memory through the pain in my head. Austin's face flashed in front of me, full of tension and unhappiness as he said he couldn't give me a ride home.

I didn't mention that part, sticking to the facts instead. "I finished practice at the rink and I decided to walk home. And..."

No matter how hard I tried, nothing else appeared. One minute, I'd been walking down the street, and the next, I woke up in this bed.

"I don't remember anything else."

Angie nodded. "That's fine. It sounds like you're doing great. We're going to give you something for the pain, and the doctor will be in soon to talk about everything, okay?"

As she turned away, I tried to raise my right hand to scratch my face and a deep, jarring pain shot through my body. With a whimpered cry, I finally looked down at the rest of my body.

A cast covered my right arm from my hand to above my elbow. Although my legs were under the blankets, the right one looked much bigger than the left, as if it had also been encased in something.

"Mom?"

Fear and panic started to take over as I looked down at the body that didn't look like mine at all. What happened? What was wrong with me?

In a second, her arms were around me. "It's okay," she whispered, repeating her words from earlier. "It's going to be fine."

"But... what... how..." I couldn't get any more words out as my throat closed, the panic almost overwhelming by that point. My mom's body shuddered against me, her tears wet against my cheek, but I couldn't cry. I simply felt numb with shock.

I needed someone to tell me what was going on, and finally, my mom pulled back, her eyes an even brighter red than before and trails of tears streaking down her face.

"It was an accident," she said, her lips trembling as she spoke. "A car jumped the curb and ran into you."

I recognized all the words but they didn't make sense to me. They couldn't be real. Slowly, my head moved back and forth in a silent 'no' because I didn't want to believe it. There must have been some mistake.

After taking a deep breath to steady herself, she continued. "Luckily, the car wasn't going too fast. You hit your head but they've done an MRI and it doesn't look like there was any damage to your brain."

Logically, I knew I should be happy about that, but I noticed she didn't say anything about the damage to my body.

My body that I needed for skating, the only thing in the world that I wanted to do.

"My leg?" I whispered, and she pressed her lips together as more tears rolled down her face.

"It's broken, honey, and your arm too. But they'll heal. You're going to be fine. You're so strong, you're going to be just fine, and I'll be right here with you."

"The season..." I started to say, but she shook her head, and my heart broke before she even said the words.

"I don't think so, sweetheart. The season's gone."

Gone? Our first year as seniors, all the momentum we had from Junior Worlds, our new program, all of it, just... gone?

Finally, my numbness shattered and the tears came; hot, bitter tears that streamed down my face as I sobbed. My mom lay down on the bed beside me as much as she could, holding me tightly while I cried longer and harder than I ever had in my life.

At that moment, I really didn't care if it could have been worse. Losing the whole skating year was the worst thing I could imagine.

When my sobs finally turned to sniffles, my body too worn out to cry any more, we lay quietly for a few more minutes before my mom got up to get me some Kleenex and a washcloth for my face.

"Can I ask you something?" she said tentatively as she finished wiping my face clean.

I nodded, even though the motion made my head ache.

"Why were you walking home? I thought Austin was going to drive you."

The thought of Austin nearly brought the tears back, even though it didn't seem possible I had any left to cry. My accident didn't just affect me. Austin would lose his whole season too. He would be stuck in limbo, waiting for me to recover, and he would hate me for it. Things between us would be worse than ever.

"Amy?" My mom prompted me again when I said nothing, lost in my spiralling doubts and fears.

"He... uh, he had something else to do. He said to take a cab, but..."

I didn't have to fill in the rest. My mom knew how shy I got around people I didn't know, and I didn't like having to take a taxi unless I absolutely had to. Rather than deal with the awkwardness, I decided to walk home instead.

"You could have called me," my mom whispered and even though I didn't look at her, I could tell she'd started crying again.

"You were working. It's not your fault, Mom."

As upset as I was over everything, I could see the situation for what it was: a terrible accident. Nobody meant for it to happen, and nobody could change it. I would just have to focus on my recovery and getting back on the ice as soon as possible. Whatever it took, I would do, there wasn't a doubt in my mind about that.

Eventually, the doctor came in and explained the extent of my injuries. He told me once again how lucky I had been. Apparently, the accident happened the day before, so I'd already been in the hospital for a whole day. He confirmed there didn't seem to be any damage to my head other than a bump and some bruising, but my leg had broken in two places, and my arm in one. They had already done surgery on my leg.

"Will there be a scar?" Picturing my skating dresses, where the audience and the judges and the cameras could all see my legs, I tried to brace myself for his answer.

"I'm afraid so."

Disappointment shot through me despite my attempts to be prepared.

"The good news is that there's no reason that you can't make a full recovery. You're young and in great shape, so with some hard work and physio rehab, we'll get you back on the ice. I'm sure of it."

That *did* make me feel better since I would be more than willing to work hard. If determination was all it took, I had nothing to worry about.

After the doctor left, I turned to my mom. "Have you talked to Austin yet?"

A scowl darkened her face. "No. I talked to Karen and your coaching team, so everyone knows what's happened. You don't need to worry about anybody else."

"But I need to tell him I'm sorry about our training..."

She shook her head, cutting me off. "You don't need to apologize to him for anything. He should be the one apologizing to you for leaving you on your own."

Although I didn't agree with her, she was close to tears again, so I let it go. Austin wasn't to blame since none of us could have ever anticipated this happening. I'd make sure he knew that when I spoke to him.

"Get some sleep now, honey. I'll leave you alone so you aren't distracted. The most important thing now is that you rest up so you can heal. We'll worry about everything else later, okay?"

I nodded my head in agreement, and as she left the room, I could have almost sworn that I caught a glimpse of Austin's jacket in the hallway as the door swung shut behind her. My heart beat a little faster in anticipation of his visit, but no one else came in, so eventually, I had to accept it must have been my imagination.

It took a while for my mind to stop replaying everything and going over everything I'd lost, but finally, I fell asleep, drifting into dreams where my leg was fine, Austin and I skated our new program perfectly, and at the end, he kissed me again, the way he had that night on my driveway.

That time, he didn't regret it at all.

~**Austin**~

~*Present day*~

By the time I got home, my confusion hadn't lessened at all, but it had started to mix with hurt and anger. Amy was there, in Toronto. She must have been there for a while if she went to university. Clearly, she knew where I was the whole time, and she must have known that she could get in touch with me whenever she wanted. Why didn't she? Why did she stay away all that time and then, when she finally did contact me, why did she pretend to be someone else?

It didn't take long to realize I'd made a complete fool of myself over the past few days. As I thought back to the things I had said to 'Mia', the things I had told her about Amy and about myself, and especially to the way I flirted with her and told her how I felt a connection with her, my whole body burned with humiliation.

Had she wanted that? Was it a way of punishing me? Maybe she was still so angry that she planned it as some form of revenge. And if she had, maybe I had no right to complain. After all, she couldn't possibly blame me any more than I blamed myself.

But I never thought she would be cruel about it. She'd never been that kind of person, at least not when I knew her.

True, I'd never apologized, but only because I never had the chance. I would have told her every day how sorry I was if she had let me.

I'd wanted nothing more than to say those words to her ever since the day it happened.

~Four years earlier~

The music thumped loudly, nearly shaking the walls of my room, but I still wanted it louder. I wanted to drown out all the thoughts in my head. Despite being home from the rink for two hours, I'd spent most of it lying there on my bed, staring up at the ceiling, and I still wasn't any closer to figuring out exactly what I would say to Amy when I saw her the next morning.

Suddenly, the room went quiet and I looked over to see that my mom had walked in and turned off my music. I hadn't even heard the door open over the sound of the pounding bass.

Expecting her to be angry or annoyed at how loud it had been, I sat up, but to my surprise, she didn't yell. If anything, she looked... nervous.

"Mom? What's going on?"

Taking a deep breath, she sat down next to me on the bed, and her continued silence made me even more worried. It wasn't like her at all.

"I just got a call from Karen," she finally said, speaking so quietly that I had to lean in closer to hear her better.

Those words confused me even more. She looked so somber, I almost thought someone had died, but Karen would only be calling about skating... or about Amy. An uncomfortable, gnawing sensation took root in my stomach, and it only got worse with the next words out of my mom's mouth.

"She just talked to Mrs Gardiner."

Damn it. It *was* about Amy. Did she say something to her mom about our kiss? Amy's mom was the only person in the world more protective of Amy than I was, and if she knew I kissed her, she'd be furious with me.

But why would she go through Karen to complain about it? I had to be missing something.

My mom took another breath, looking down at her hands, and I reached over to take one of her hands in mine, trying to spur her on. "You're scaring me, Mom. Just tell me."

Not knowing seemed worse than knowing, whatever it might be.

At least I thought so, until she finally blurted it out.

"Amy's in the hospital."

For a moment, the room seemed to spin around me.

That couldn't be right. There must have been some mistake. Amy had been at the rink with me and afterwards, she went home. She should have been hanging out in her room, probably worrying about the situation between us, just like me.

When my mom lifted her head to see my reaction, the redness around her eyes shocked me. My mom didn't even like Amy, everyone knew it, so what would have made her so upset?

"What happened?" I managed to ask, though I couldn't be sure how I put the words together.

"Apparently, there was an accident on the way home from the rink. They don't know how bad it is yet. She's in surgery right now."

I stared at her blankly as my mind tried to make sense of any of that. Without even realizing I meant to do it, I got to my feet and headed towards the door.

"Where are you going?" my mom asked, also getting to her feet and grabbing hold of my arm.

"I have to see her." I didn't understand anything else, but I knew that with certainty.

"You can't. They're operating on her right now and they'll only be letting family in, at least for a while."

I wanted to disagree and point out that Amy and I were closer than family, but even in my agitated state, I knew she had a point. I couldn't do anything at the hospital and they probably wouldn't even let me in. Even so, staying in my room and doing nothing also seemed impossible.

"What kind of accident?" I asked next, still trying to make sense of everything.

As soon as the words were out of my mouth, a thought came into my head, followed by a wave of nausea.

No. It couldn't be. Please, no.

My next words were just a whisper. "Was it the taxi?"

I told her to take a taxi home. I was supposed to drive her, and I told her to take a cab instead. Did I do this? Was it my fault?

"I don't know any of the details. Karen didn't know much."

My stomach churned violently at even the possibility that I had caused Amy any kind of pain. Pushing past my mom, I stumbled down the hall to the bathroom and retched into the toilet. Nothing came out, but I couldn't stop my body from trying anyway, trying to rid itself of the guilt and horror inside.

My mom must have followed me because her hand rubbed my back as I bent uselessly over the toilet. "I'll take you to see her as soon as you're allowed."

My mom's out-of-character kindness only made me feel worse. She wouldn't have acted so nice unless things were really bad.

The rest of that night passed in a blur. My mom called Karen back, begging her to update us as soon as she knew anything else. At close to midnight, we received a call saying that Amy had come out of surgery but hadn't woken up yet. Apparently, she had some broken bones and they were watching her for concussion or a more serious brain injury.

Sleep was impossible but I kept trying anyway. Even the worst nightmare would be better than what I felt while awake and the constant drumming of three words in my head: *It's my fault.*

If I hadn't refused to drive her, if I hadn't kissed her the night before, if I hadn't let myself fall for her in the first place, none of it would have happened. *If, if, if.* The word kept repeating in my head all night long, accusing me and demanding retribution.

I didn't sleep at all.

The next morning, I went to the hospital as soon as it opened for visiting hours. Although I knew I would have to wait to see her, I didn't care. I couldn't be anywhere else.

Close to noon, I finally saw Amy's dad when he came out one of the doors, heading towards the cafeteria and I quickly intercepted him.

"Mr Gardiner?"

Bloodshot, red eyes looked over at me, not really seeing me. "Austin?" His confusion mirrored how I felt as he blinked, trying to bring me into focus. "What are you doing here?"

"I need to see Amy. How is she?"

He nodded slowly, as if he couldn't process anything at a normal speed. "She's doing okay, but she's still not awake. I'm just going to get some food for her mom, but you can come back with me afterwards if you want."

I quickly agreed and went with him to the cafeteria to pick up some lunch for him and Mrs Gardiner. We arrived back at the door to Amy's room just as Mrs Gardiner came out of it. Her expression quickly darkened as she caught sight of me.

"What are you doing here?"

The anger in her voice caught me off guard. Amy's mom had always been friendly towards me and she'd certainly never looked at me or spoken to me like that before. I couldn't blame her for being upset, though. The situation was terrible.

"How's Amy?" I asked, pushing aside my own feelings. She was the only thing that mattered.

"She's going to be okay."

A huge weight lifted from my shoulders, but only until she spoke again and it settled right back down.

"No thanks to you."

"Meredith!" Mr Gardiner sounded shocked as he stared at his wife. "Austin didn't do anything."

"No, he didn't," Mrs Gardiner agreed, keeping her bitter eyes full of hurt and resentment trained on me. "All he had to do was drive her home, and he couldn't even do that."

Her words hit me like a ton of bricks, the weight of them causing me to take a step back. *Oh, God.* I'd been right. All of it was my fault.

"It was an accident," Mr Gardiner argued, trying to defend me even though I didn't deserve it. "Blaming anyone doesn't help."

His words seemed to bounce right off Amy's mom as if she hadn't heard them. Her furious gaze remained directed at me. "She needs to rest now. When she's ready to see you, we'll let you know. Until then, don't bother to come back."

As I blinked, two tears ran down my cheeks. I wasn't sure when I started crying, but in the face of her mother's anger and my own culpability, I knew that I had to do what was best for Amy. If she needed space and time to rest, I would give it to her. I would wait until she wanted to see me.

I could only hope that I wouldn't have to wait too long.

Chapter Ten

~Amelia~

~Present day~

Eventually, the taxi arrived to pick me up from outside the rink and take me back to my dorm room. I stared out the window the whole time, trying to decide what to do next. Trying to deal with my memories and my emotions around Austin proved impossible, so I focused on the article instead, which also had my stomach in knots.

What if Austin complained about me to the magazine? Would the article be shelved, making all of this subterfuge for nothing? The best way I could think of to avoid that would be to apologize to him and ask him not to say anything, even if the idea of asking Austin for a favour made me feel nearly as sick as the idea of losing my job.

Still, I had to own my mistake. I screwed up and, like it or not, Austin held my future at the magazine in his hands. At least I had his phone number, which I counted as a blessing in a situation that sorely lacked any other ones. It would allow me to get in touch with him without having to talk to him or see him again.

After I typed out the text, I stared at it for a couple of minutes, reading and rereading it until the words barely made sense anymore.

> Hi. I know you must be angry with me, and I'm sorry I wasn't up front with you. It's a long story, but I didn't want anything to distract from the profile I'm writing. I'm serious about making this feature as good as possible. I'll send it to you before I submit it so you'll know exactly what I've written.

It felt impersonal, but that had been my intent. The article didn't have anything to do with us or the past, and at that point, the only thing we had in common *was* my article.

Even so, I couldn't help adding one more sentence.

> Good luck in Seattle next week.

I hit send before I could change my mind.

For the rest of the day, every time I heard any sound, no matter how different it sounded from my message alert, I nervously pulled out my phone to check it. Austin read the text shortly after I sent it but he didn't respond.

I had absolutely no idea what he thought about the whole mess.

The next day, I had class in the morning and afterwards, I met up with Gaby to head over to the magazine office. As we walked, I filled her in on the previous day's events.

She let out a low whistle when I finished, looking at me with her eyebrows drawn together in concern. "What are you going to do now?"

"I'm going to write the article and send it to him. Hopefully, he'll be happy with it and that'll be the end of it. Everything can go back to normal."

"You really think so? What about him asking you out?"

"That happened before he figured out who I am. Since he hasn't even responded to my text yet, I'm pretty sure he never wants to see me again."

The thought made my stomach ache, even though it had been my plan since the beginning to do the article and not look back. Gaby shrugged, and I couldn't be sure if that meant she agreed with me or not.

Once we arrived at the magazine's office, I sat down at my desk and pulled out my recorder and the notes I had made from my interviews with Austin. The idea of listening to them again and reliving everything we'd talked about felt like adding another bruise to my already battered heart, but getting the article written and over with would be the only way to move past all of it.

No sooner had I arranged everything how I wanted it when Anna, the editor's assistant, stopped by my desk.

"Hey, Mia. There's someone here to see you, he's been waiting for a while. I put him in Samantha's office since she's out for the afternoon."

He? Oh, no. *No, no, no.*

It couldn't be.

But on the other hand, who else would be looking for me at the magazine? As improbable as it seemed, nothing else made sense.

Anxiety settled in my stomach like a ball of lead as I stood up and followed Anna to the editor's office. Through the window, I caught a glimpse of the man inside, and even though I could only see the back of his head as he sat in one of the plastic bucket chairs, I recognized him immediately.

Austin was sitting in the editor's office at Urban Style magazine and I had no choice but to speak to him, with him knowing exactly who I was. The confrontation I'd done my best to avoid for a week was about to happen, ready or not.

Coming to a halt and pressing myself against the wall so he wouldn't see me if he turned his head, I tried to get more information from Anna. "What did he say when he got here? What does he want?"

She kept walking, unaware that I'd stopped. "He said he wanted to talk to you about the piece you're writing."

"Did he seem angry?"

Hearing my voice further behind her than she expected, Anna turned back, her head tilting curiously. "No. Why? What happened?"

Explaining the situation to her didn't appeal to me at all, so I quickly shook my head. "It's nothing. It's fine. Can I talk to him in there?"

"Go ahead. Samantha won't be back today." She gave me an encouraging smile. "You've got this."

If only she had any idea how much I did *not* have this.

After thanking her, I took a deep breath and tried to steady myself. I'd done things that scared me before. Stepping out onto the ice in front of tens of thousands of people for the first time had been a little terrifying, but even then, my heart never pounded quite as loud as it did when I turned the handle to open the door and walked into Samantha's office.

Austin immediately looked up, his phone in his hands. How long had he been waiting? Anna said 'a while', but that covered a pretty wide range of time. As his eyes landed on me, he stood up, sliding the phone into his pocket and turning to give me his full attention.

"Hi."

My greeting couldn't have sounded much weaker as I searched his face for some indication of exactly how angry he was. Uncharacteristically, his eyes looked cold, and his nostrils flared at the singular word I spoke. Those didn't look like good signs, especially when coupled with the fact that he didn't respond. He appeared to be waiting for me to say something else.

Trying to ease the tension, I cleared my throat. "Do you want something to drink? Water, coffee?"

His eyes narrowed, letting me know if I hadn't guessed it already that he didn't come there to have a pleasant chat.

When he finally spoke, his voice came out low and hard. "Was this some kind of game? Were you trying to make me look like an idiot?"

I winced, trying to swallow down the lump in my throat. His anger couldn't be clearer, and the worst part was that he was completely justified in feeling it. More than anything, he probably felt embarrassed, both that he hadn't recognized me and that he'd hit on me. If he had known my real identity, he never would have asked me out.

I tried my best to keep my tone conciliatory. "Of course it wasn't a game, and I certainly don't think you're an idiot. I wanted to keep the focus on you, and I thought it would be a distraction if you knew it was me. I didn't want to make it about us."

"So the hair, the glasses, the name, all of this..." He waved his hand over me, indicating my whole appearance. "You did this for the story?"

I shook my head, forcing my next words out a little more strongly. "No, not at all. This is me now, this is who I am. As I said in my text, it's a long story, but the important part is that I really am sorry for misleading you. I would still like to write the profile, and I hope you're okay with that. I promise I'll write the best article I can."

He pressed his lips together, his nostrils flaring again. "That's not the important part, Amy. I don't care about the profile. Why are you pretending to be someone else? Giving me a fake name? Where the hell have you been for the last four years?"

The pain I could see simmering in his eyes both hurt and confused me.

"I'm not 'pretending'," I shot back at him, my own pain pushing through my nerves on its way back to the surface. "I needed a fresh start. When I couldn't skate anymore, it felt like my life was over. It took me a long time to be ready to move on and it didn't help when people would recognize me. I started going by Mia instead of Amy, still short for Amelia. My mom and I both took her maiden name after my dad left. I'm Mia Wilson now; it's not a fake name, it's who I am."

Austin watched me carefully, listening intently to everything. "Your dad left?"

Out of all the things I said, *that* was the one he focused on? I nodded, not wanting to get drawn into the details of it.

"And your voice? The accent?" The anger in his tone faded a little, replaced with simple confusion.

"We lived in Newfoundland for a while. My mom's still there. A lot of things have changed."

That was a massive understatement, and he knew it. A long moment of silence followed my explanation, both of us feeling the weight of it. With so many questions and so many things left unsaid, neither of us knew where to start. It seemed easier to say nothing at all.

When he spoke again, his tone had softened even further, and he stuck to the one subject that had always been a safe topic for us in the past: dancing.

"Why aren't you skating? You're still amazing. That Paso Doble we did the other day was good. Really good."

Tears sprang to my eyes, burning the back of them, and I looked away, clenching my jaw to keep them from showing. How could he ask me that with a straight face? And he said *I* was the one playing games?

"It's hard to dance without a partner."

That was all I could get out, but no other words were needed. We both lapsed into silence again, and because I kept my gaze focused on the city outside Samantha's window, I had no idea what his reaction to my words had been.

He didn't defend himself, or offer any explanation as to why he abandoned me. Maybe he felt, like I did, that dredging all of it back up at that point wouldn't accomplish anything.

So, even though I could have explained further, although I could have told him exactly how much he hurt me, although my blood felt it might reach a boiling point within my veins, I pushed it all down to focus on the immediate issue between us as I turned back to him.

"I don't want to bring any drama into your life. That's exactly what I was trying *not* to do. You've got a lot going on and you don't need any distractions, so I apologize, again, for not being honest with you. At this point, I've got everything I need for the article and as I said, I'll send it to you so you can review it before I submit it. If you think I've been unfair or gotten anything wrong, let me know. Otherwise, we don't need to see each other or talk to each other again. Once the article's published, you can forget all about me."

Again, I added in my mind. You can forget about me *again*.

"You really think that's what I want, Amy?"

He took a step towards me, and I took one back, out of some kind of self-preservation instinct.

"Mia," I reminded him. "It's Mia now."

His head shook, his dark hair swishing over his forehead as it did. "Not to me. You'll always be my Amy."

His Amy? Since when?

"And you owe me more than that," he added.

Anger bubbled up in me again and he must have been able to see it on my face. *I* owed *him*? He couldn't be serious.

If my anger intimidated him, he didn't show it. Instead, he elaborated on his statement. "You want to make it up to me for lying to me? At the very least, you owe me a dance."

What in the world was he talking about? "We already danced the other day."

"I know you've got more than that."

His words sent a shiver through me, completely against my will. They sounded like a threat and a promise, all at once. How did he manage to make me feel so many different things at the same time?

"One session, just you and me. Alone."

Somehow, he made the prospect of dancing with him sound dangerous and appealing at the same time. My whole world seemed to be on the verge of spinning out of control, so I tried to grab onto something concrete. "And if I agree, you won't say anything about the article? About me?"

If he was going to insist, I could at least make sure I got something out of it too.

He nodded in agreement, his eyes still fixed on me. "If that's what you want, I'll keep your secret. As long as you dance with me."

~Austin~

I hoped that seeing Amy would help to clear things up but I left the magazine office feeling nearly as confused as when I came in.

The text she sent me only made me angrier. Although she apologized, she didn't give me any explanation, no clue at all as to why she came to me pretending to be someone else. She only wanted to talk about the article, as if that mattered at all compared to everything else we needed to talk about.

In her office, she told me that she hadn't been pretending, at least not in the way I thought. Apparently, she had adopted this whole other persona, and I still didn't have the first idea why that would have been necessary.

She wanted to move on, fine, I supposed I could understand that, but why would she need to change *everything* about herself?

She still looked different, but now that I knew what to look for, I could see Amy there too. In some ways, I didn't know how I ever missed it. Besides the physical similarities, other little habits stood out to me too, like her nervous habit of reaching for her four-leaf clover whenever she felt uncertain about something, for instance. She'd done that as Mia, her hand going to her neck out of instinct, but without the chain hanging there, I hadn't put the pieces together.

At least one thing had become clear: I finally knew why 'Mia' had been so insistent on pushing me away when I tried to get close to her. She must have still blamed me for everything that happened.

She wanted nothing to do with me beyond her article.

That wasn't what I wanted, though. If nothing else, I wanted to apologize and finally clear the air between us. I could have insisted we do it right there in that random office in a city that had no memories for either of us, but it didn't seem right.

We should talk on the ice. Our safe space, where we could be fully ourselves, it had always been the place where things made sense for us.

For that reason, I insisted that we dance together again.

Well, for that reason, and also just because I wanted to dance with her. Dancing with Mia felt good, but now that I knew I'd actually been dancing with Amy, I wanted to enjoy it properly. I wanted to pay attention to every part of having her beside me again, even if only for one last time.

Doing it at my club where my mother or Grace or anyone else could see us would be asking for trouble, but when I asked Amy if she knew somewhere else we could go, she surprised me by saying that she had some private ice time and I could join her for it. She gave me the address and told me to arrive at 5:30 the next morning, and I held onto the promise of seeing her again for the rest of the day.

The next morning, I got up even earlier than usual, arrived at the rink a few minutes ahead of time and knocked on the door, my bag slung over my shoulder in the chilly morning air. An older man with grey hair opened the door and his mouth fell open when he saw me.

"Austin Black! I can't believe it. It's been a long time." He pulled me into a hug before I could react, but when my brain caught up, I realized exactly who he was.

"I didn't know you were here, Terry."

Terry used to drive Amy to our rink in Ottawa when Amy's parents were working, before I got my license and started driving her myself. On the days when Terry drove her, he often hung out watching our practice, like my mom did, but also not at all like my mom did.

While my mom stood at the boards with our coach, insisting she be included in every decision, Terry sat in the stands, watching it all but never saying a word other than telling us afterwards that we were doing a great job. I had to admit he hadn't crossed my mind very many times over the last few years, but seeing him at the rink that morning was a genuine pleasure.

"How did you end up here?" I asked him while I sat down in the stands to get my skates on.

Four rows of seats lined one side of the community rink with benches for the hockey players on the other side. It had been a long time since I skated in a rink that wasn't dedicated solely to figure skating. Local hockey team championship banners hung at the end of the arena next to the large scoreboard that also acted as the clock. Five thirty-two, it said, and Amy was already out on the ice. She didn't come over or acknowledge my arrival, looking lost in her own world.

While Terry told me about his retirement and his move to Toronto, I kept my eyes on Amy, my fingers doing up my laces on muscle memory. Under my gaze, she double sculled around the ice, her body bouncing as her knees bent to judge the way the ice reacted to her that morning.

Everything about it felt achingly familiar, sending a pang of loss stuttering through my chest. I had watched her do that a thousand times or more, every time we started a warm-up.

That morning, she'd pulled her hair back and removed her glasses, making her look a lot more like the Amy I remembered. She had grown another inch or two, and her chest had gotten a little bigger, but other than that, she looked exactly like the girl I'd always found so appealing.

How much had she changed on the inside, though? That was one of the questions I hoped to answer that morning.

With my skates laced up, I said goodbye to Terry and let myself onto the ice. I gave a few test pushes, noting how the ice felt more brittle than my usual rink before I began my warm-up. With long strokes, pushing as hard as I could into the ice, I flew around the edges of the rink, rushing past Amy who still didn't even look at me.

That was normal too, though. I had my own routine and she had hers, we'd always done it that way. We'd warm up individually first before warming up together.

Did she remember that warm-up too? Would she do it with me?

Testing the waters, I skated up alongside her when I'd finished my individual warm-up, the blood pumping through my veins and my heart having found its steady rhythm. Wordlessly, I held out my hand to her, and though she didn't look at me or say anything in response, she slid her hand into mine as if it belonged there.

When we stepped again, we were in perfect sync.

Hand-in-hand, we stroked around the ice twice before switching to a Kilian hold, my right arm behind her back and my hand holding hers over her hip as we went through all the familiar steps. It didn't take much for me to remember what to do since I'd taught the same warm-up to Grace. We made a few changes over the years, but the basics remained the same. Doing it with Amy rather than Grace felt different in a way I couldn't quite put into words.

It felt like coming home.

Aware that we still hadn't spoken to each other, I finally broke the silence.

"I brought some music. I thought we could do some of the pattern dances to find our rhythm. Do you have a preference?"

She shook her head, still not making eye contact. "You can choose."

I recognized the measured tone and clipped words of her reply, since they were exactly the way I spoke when I wanted to keep distance between myself and another person. Maybe I learned that from her.

There were so many parts of her that had left an impression on me.

We did the Viennese Waltz first, followed by the Midnight Blues. Amy stumbled a couple of times on the steps or the timings, but I held her tightly in my arms until she was able to catch up again. For someone who hadn't been training properly for the last four years, she was still amazingly impressive, not that it surprised me at all.

"Why aren't you skating?" I asked her again as we finished the Blues and I released her, both of us gliding along to catch our breath. "You obviously still love it."

She told me the day before that she couldn't skate without a partner, but that didn't really answer the question. All I knew was that after her accident, she went somewhere to recover. My mom didn't want me to lose the training time, so after a couple of weeks, she found me a temporary partner to train with until Amy was well enough to be back on the ice.

That partner was Grace.

Almost six months after the accident, my mom told me that she'd spoken to Karen who said that Amy wasn't coming back. Her injuries had healed to the point where she could have, but she decided not to.

I couldn't believe it. I didn't *want* to. How could she give up something that she loved so much? I wished that I could ask her myself, that I could talk to her and try to understand her reasoning, but I hadn't heard a single word from her during those six months.

With only her cell phone to contact her, I sent her text after text during that time. At first, I asked how she felt and how she was coping with her injuries, but when she didn't respond to those messages, I just started telling her things instead, talking to her as I would have done on the ice. A day rarely went by without me sending some kind of message, but she never replied or even read the messages.

The only reason I could think of for her silence was that she blamed me for what had happened, just like her mom did, and was angry with me for putting her in the position that caused her accident in the first place. Still, I never stopped hoping that one day she would change her mind and write me back.

"Maybe that's why she's not coming back," my mom suggested gently when she broke the news to me and I questioned why Amy would ever quit. "Maybe she just doesn't want to be your partner anymore."

With those words ringing in my ears, I went into my room and cried for the loss of my partner, the future we'd dreamed of together, and my friend.

Although it wasn't the first time I cried about the whole situation since Amy's accident, it would be the last. As much as I hated to admit it, my mom was right. If Amy decided to quit, I had to accept it and move on.

I didn't send any more texts.

A couple of weeks later, we moved to Toronto to train with Grace permanently at the club where we still skated. I assumed that if Amy still wanted to skate, just not with me, she would have found another partner too. Since I never heard that she did, I began to think she had simply lost her love of the sport after the accident. With nothing else to go on, I had to invent my own reasons to explain her disappearance not only from my life but from the skating world in general.

However, seeing her on the ice that morning, and after the week I'd just spent with her as Mia, I could see that she still had the passion and talent she'd always had, so obviously, I'd missed something.

Why did she stop?

Amy glanced over at me with a pained expression, her response stiff. "I tried a few other partners but it never felt right. I didn't want to waste my time on something that wasn't going anywhere."

Her direct, no-nonsense answer brought a smile to my face, but only for a second until the meaning of her words sunk in. If she hadn't wanted to stop skating in general, then she must have simply wanted to stop skating with *me*.

"We've only got a few more minutes," she said, gesturing to the large scoreboard clock at the end of the rink. "A hockey practice will be starting soon. Did you want to do anything else before we go?"

I absolutely did. She might not like it, but since this would probably be my only chance, I intended to ask for it anyway.

During one of our interviews, she asked me if I had a favourite program, and I told her the truth: my favourite program was the last one we worked on together, the one she created for us. The best program that I never got to perform, and the program that meant more to me than all the other ones put together.

Looking straight into her pale blue eyes, I made my request. "I want to do your program. I want to skate The Last 5 Years."

Chapter Eleven

~Amelia~

My stomach flipped as soon as the words left Austin's mouth. For years, I'd imagined what it would feel like to do that program again and there he stood, offering to skate it with me. *Demanding* it, even.

Why did he insist on this whole morning, on skating with me again? What was the point? We knew we were good together; no one had ever doubted it. He wouldn't leave Grace to train with me again, not when they were months away from an Olympic medal and he'd been the one to walk away in the first place. Changing partners at this point would be insane.

So, what *was* the point? I kept coming back to that question, unable to find an answer that didn't involve cruelty on his part. Was it some kind of revenge for me hiding my identity from him? A way to pour salt in the wound of my ruined dreams?

That didn't sound like the Austin I knew, but the man in front of me, so familiar in so many ways, was a stranger in others, and I had to admit I didn't have the first idea what was going through his head at that moment.

"I don't know if I remember it," I said softly, looking down at the ice instead of at him.

"Liar."

The word could have sounded harsh, but it didn't. Instead, it almost sounded... affectionate. When I looked back at him, his eyes were fixed on me.

"You could do it in your sleep."

I could have disagreed, but it would have been a lie. I *did* do the program in my sleep, even now. In my dreams, Austin and I competed at our first senior Worlds using that program. The sound of our blades slicing the ice as we did it, the applause from the crowd, and the sound of the national anthem playing as we stood on the podium formed the soundtrack that played over and over in my head like a worn-out record. I had dreamt every moment of it more times than I could count, so many times that sometimes, I could almost believe it had actually happened.

When I didn't argue, he pulled out his phone and skated over to the boards, calling over to Terry. I kept an eye on him as I circled the ice, trying to figure out what he was up to. After handing his phone to Terry, he went to his speaker next, cuing up another piece of music. When he skated back to me, determination lined every sharp edge of his face.

It had been all I could do not to break down when he asked me yet again why I didn't skate any more. It must have been so easy for him to replace me that he assumed I could just go out and get another partner too, no problem.

And I *did* try. When I found out that he had broken our partnership and would be skating with Grace permanently, I tried to move on. What I told him that morning was true, though: I couldn't find the same connection with anyone else. That feeling of being in tune with the other person eluded me. My new coach tried to tell me that it would come over time, that it would just be a matter of working with the new partner until that connection formed, but I remembered the way it felt with Austin the very first time we skated together. It might not have been perfect, but it felt *right*, and I wanted that feeling.

If I couldn't have it, it seemed better not to skate competitively at all rather than feel its absence every time I got on the ice.

For a while, I hoped that, even though Austin had made the choice to skate with Grace, he would eventually get in touch with me, just to reconnect. My mom assured me that she gave Karen and Austin's mom my new phone number, since my phone had been destroyed in the accident and I no longer had his number.

Since I never heard from him, I could only assume he wanted to make a clean break.

Which led me back to my main question: what exactly did he want out of skating with me that morning?

"Terry's going to film us," Austin said as he reached me back in the centre of the ice, gesturing over to where Terry stood at the boards, holding Austin's phone.

A new feeling of unease rose in me. "Why?"

"It's an amazing program. I want to show it to our choreographer."

"You are not doing that program with Grace." The refusal rushed out of me before I even had a chance to think it through. Bitterness laced every word, catching me off guard with its strength. I didn't resent Grace, I understood none of what happened was her fault, but the idea of her dancing the steps I'd created for Austin and I to do together set off a jealousy and possessiveness in me that I didn't even know I possessed.

Austin obviously heard it too because he recoiled, his eyes wide, looking chagrined. "Of course not. I wouldn't do that, Amy. That program is ours. But there might be elements…"

That didn't make it any better. In fact, it might even make it worse. "So, you want to cut it up? Use it for scraps?"

Feeling the familiar burning starting behind my eyes, I turned away, determined not to let him see just how emotional I felt. How did he still have the power to stir my emotions so deeply? I thought I'd grown stronger than that.

After all those years, I should have.

Austin came up behind me, his hands gently gripping my upper arms. "I'm messing this up, again. That didn't come out right. I won't use anything from it if you don't want me to, but I'll be honest with you: I want people to see it. They should know how talented you are, not just as a skater, but as a choreographer. That program deserves to see the light of day."

His words helped to mollify me somewhat, not so much because of what he said but because of the sincerity in them. It sounded so much like how he always encouraged me before, how he always backed me up and believed in me, even when no one else did.

"If you don't want me to show anyone, I won't," he repeated. "The recording will just be for me. I'd like to be able to watch it, as my own memento and nothing else. Please skate it with me, just this one time. For us."

My resolve weakened with his pleading, not only for his sake but because I *wanted* to skate it. I wanted to remember how it felt to do it with him, and pretend, for four and a half minutes, that nothing had changed.

Pretend that we still had a promising future in front of us.

Pretend that there was still an 'us' at all.

"Alright," I agreed quietly, my back still to him as I gave in. "One time."

~Four years earlier~

Our group of five sat around the table at Austin's house: me and my mom on one side of the table, my dad on the other, Mrs Black at the head of the table and Austin at the other end, next to me. What should have been a friendly back-to-training dinner had grown uncomfortably tense.

Austin had just announced that we wanted to use the free dance I created as our official competition program for our first year as senior ice dancers.

My mom beamed with pride. My dad smiled too, always supportive of me but never involved in the details. No matter how much he tried, he never found a real passion for, or even understanding of, the sport.

Mrs Black, on the other hand, knew it inside out, and she glowered at me from the end of the table.

"This is your first year as seniors," she reminded us stiffly. "You need to be taken seriously. This is not a time for some second-rate amateur…"

"Mom." Austin cut her off with an impressive glare of his own. "Amy has been fixing things in our programs for years. She knows what she's doing."

"If she hadn't fixed that spin at Junior Worlds, they would have been downgraded," my mom pointed out. "It would have cost them the gold."

"Be that as it may, there's a big difference between pointing out technical problems and designing a whole program," Mrs Black continued, refusing to grant me even the slightest acknowledgement. "We pay a professional choreographer for a reason."

"Amy's better than the choreographer we had last year," Austin said mildly, stretching his arm out to take my hand in his, giving a visual confirmation of his support to everyone else in the room. "Her program is the best one we've ever had."

Mrs Black's eyes rested on me with a look I could only describe as contempt. "You all need to stop puffing up her ego so much. It's no wonder she thinks she's so much better than everyone else when you…"

Not waiting to hear the rest of what she had to say, I jumped up and left the room, running into the bathroom down the hall and shutting the door behind me. On the ice, I would have stood up to her and proven to her that I knew what I was talking about, but in her house, with her glaring at me as if I was still the little girl she first met three years earlier, I couldn't help worrying that she had a point.

No one choreographed their own programs, not at our level. As Junior World champions, there would be a lot of pressure on us to do well in our first senior season. What if the program made us look childish by comparison with the other, professionally-choreographed programs? What if...

"Amy?" Austin's voice drifted in from the other side of the door, accompanied by a soft knock. "You okay?"

Sighing, I opened the door to find him leaning against the wall outside with a half-smile that brought out his dimple, and my stomach flipped. Similar to his mother, Austin affected me differently off the ice than he did on it. When we skated, when I was in the zone, he was simply my partner, my slightly goofy, very talented colleague.

But there, in his home, his smile felt different. It felt like he might be more than just my partner, that the possibility existed that we could be more to each other.

"Don't listen to her," he advised, his voice firm but not without sympathy. "We knew she wasn't going to like it, remember? It's not her call."

I crossed my arms to try to both look and feel more in control. "Why does she hate me so much?"

He chuckled softly. "She doesn't like sharing the limelight. I think she's jealous of you more than anything."

I found that hard to believe, but I liked the fact that Austin thought I might be someone worth being jealous of. "I don't really want to go back out there yet," I confessed.

"You don't have to. Come with me instead. There's something I've been wanting to show you."

Without waiting for my reply, he turned in the opposite direction and walked away down the hall while I trailed after him curiously. I'd only been to his house a handful of times before and I'd never seen any of the rooms in the direction he headed. He stepped into one of the open doorways and I followed after him, stopping just inside the door as I realized he'd brought me to his bedroom.

This room had played a role in my daydreams more than once, and I could barely believe I actually got to see it in real life. Curiously, my eyes scanned the room, looking for any similarities between my fantasy version and the real thing. It was messier than I expected, for one thing. Crumpled sheets covered the unmade bed, and I blushed as I took it in, images of him lying in it, shirtless and relaxed, flitting through my mind.

Austin didn't move towards the bed. Instead, he headed for his dresser, rummaging around in one of the drawers. Finding what he wanted, he pulled out a clipping from an old newspaper and held it out to me.

Expecting that he would bring it over to me, I stayed at the door, but he simply raised his eyebrows, a teasing smile playing on his lips until I walked over, avoiding the piles of clothes and other belongings strewn across the floor, and took it from his hands.

The yellowed newsprint contained an article from six years earlier about a skating camp that I'd attended in the Rocky Mountains, and I frowned at it, trying to guess why he had it and why he would be showing it to me. A photo took up half of the space on the page, showing all the skaters in our costumes for the end-of-camp show, with me and my old partner, Derrick, front and centre. We looked so tiny, probably because we were only ten years old when that photo was taken.

When I looked up at Austin curiously, his smile had widened, but it felt softer and gentler than his usual playful grin.

"You still don't see me, do you?"

My heart beating faster, I looked back at the photo. Had he been there too? I didn't remember seeing him and he never mentioned it.

Sure enough, when I looked closer, I found him in the back row, half hidden between two taller boys.

"I didn't know you were there," I exclaimed, raising my head again.

"I know. You were so focused. Even though you were just a little kid, you were so serious about the whole thing. I just went to have some fun and hang out with some of the guys from my club, but I got there early one day and you were out on the ice with a couple of other kids. Your partner wasn't there, only you, and from the way you moved, the way you connected with the ice, hearing the music in your head, I could see how much you loved it. It made me want to try harder. To be better."

He'd never told me any of that before, and my eyes searched his, looking for some clue as to why he kept it a secret for so long and why he decided to tell me about it that night.

"I kept tabs on you afterwards, and when your partner decided to stop skating and you needed a new one... well, I insisted that we go try out, even though I already had a partner at the time."

My eyes got so wide, they almost watered. When we started skating together, he told me his partner had quit, just like mine had. It felt like fate that we were both looking for new partners at the same time.

Maybe fate had less to do with it than I realized? Maybe Austin had given fate a helping hand.

"Her mom and my mom were friends," he continued. "They're not anymore, mostly because we broke up our partnership so I could skate with you. That's part of the reason my mom has always been a bit cold towards you. It's not anything you did. It's my fault, and I'm sorry that you have to deal with the fall-out."

Once again, I looked back down at the photo, studying the faces of the other kids. They were all strangers to me despite us having spent three weeks together at that camp. I could remember every step of the program we skated, but I barely spoke to the other skaters, my focus entirely on the ice even at that age.

Skating had been the most important thing in my life for as long as I could remember.

Only my feelings for Austin himself had ever come close to matching that passionate intensity, and those were still a carefully-guarded secret.

Gently, he took the clipping back from me and laid it back in his drawer before turning to face me again. "I always knew you were special on the ice and I'm so lucky to be the one who gets to skate with you. We're going to skate your program, no matter what my mom says, and when we do, everyone will finally see what I saw on that morning. They'll see just how impressive you really are."

~Austin~
~Present day~

Once Amy agreed to dance, I held out my hand to her. She slid her right hand into mine while her left hand went to the chain around her neck, touching the four-leaf clover. In that one simple gesture, she told me without any words at all exactly how nervous she felt about doing the program again. To be honest, I felt it too. In my head, I'd skated each step hundreds of times, but to be standing there with her on the ice, to have her hand in mine and know that we were actually going to perform it, felt utterly surreal. I had to keep from pinching myself to make sure it was really happening.

Silently, we moved to the centre of the ice and turned away from each other, our hands still locked together. She got up on her toes, leaning away from me, while I bent down in the opposite direction, taking up our starting position, waiting for the music to begin.

The music for this program came from one of Amy's favourite musicals, The Last 5 Years. When we started working on the program, she made me watch the movie version with her so that I would understand the story she wanted to tell. Technically, it was a love story, but it came with a twist.

The two people in the story, Jamie and Cathy, each told the story of their relationship from their own point of view. The twist was that Jamie told the story from the beginning to the end, while Cathy started at the end and worked backwards to the beginning. The only time in the show when they were at the same point in time was in the middle, at their wedding.

The story didn't end happily. The characters grew apart and got divorced, which was made clear in the very first song where Cathy lamented the end of the relationship.

Although I found the movie thought-provoking at the time, it seemed even more poignant with our years apart behind us. Being on the ice with Amy after everything we'd been through, I could identify with Cathy's part more than ever.

Knowing how our story ended, it was hard to remember how beautiful it had once been.

The opening chords blasted from my Bluetooth speaker on the boards and our bodies knew just what to do. I pulled Amy to me, propelling her backwards into my arms, pulling her back to the past, and she pushed away, pulling me along with her to the future.

The particular song Amy chose was called "Goodbye Until Tomorrow". Although it came at the end of the movie, in the song, Cathy had just finished their first date. She almost bubbled over with excitement about the connection they shared and the possibilities for their future.

Meanwhile, Jamie had reached the end of the relationship, all his optimism long faded away. When he sang goodbye, it was for the last time.

They couldn't be more at odds or their emotions any more contradictory, and Amy poured all of that emotion into every move she choreographed.

We hadn't done the dance together for four years, and we didn't put a single step wrong.

Every time I stepped, I knew where her foot would be. Every time she reached for me or I reached for her, I found her exactly where I expected her to be.

As the singers wove their tale of a partnership that was destined to fail, I threw everything I felt into the movement of my body, and Amy did the same. It had never felt so passionate before, so full of emotion, so much like we were two parts of the same whole.

As we skated, I couldn't help wondering: where were Amy and I along our journey? Was this our ending, or could it be a new beginning?

Somehow, it felt like both.

The dance ended with me on my knees, Amy in my arms, my head resting against her chest as her head fell backwards.

The music ended and silence took its place, punctuated only by our heavy breathing and Terry's whoops and cheers from the stands.

I didn't move, not wanting the connection between us to end. With each inhale and heavy exhale, I waited for Amy to get up, but she stayed where she was too. Her body trembled and so did my arms from holding her, but still, we didn't let go.

Just when it felt like I might drop her if my arms shook any more, she raised her head, tears gathered in the corner of her eyes. Blinking, I realized mine were just the same. It felt like they sprang from the same source, we were that connected. She had to have felt it too.

Pushing her back up so she could stand, I let her go and stretched my arms out. Still, neither of us skated away, or spoke. No words could capture exactly what just happened between us.

Finally, Terry called out from the boards, breaking the spell. "I'm really sorry, Amy, Austin, but I've got to start the flood now."

Amy moved first, turning away and skating over to the door as I followed close behind. "Sorry, Terry. I forgot the time."

"It's no problem," he assured both of us, looking between us with a happy smile. "You guys are welcome here anytime. That was beautiful."

He seemed to be tearing up as well as he handed my phone back to me. While he headed off towards the Zamboni, Amy and I sat down in the stands to remove our skates. Her fingers flew, unlacing her skates as quickly as possible, while I simply sat there, pulling up the video on my phone.

When Amy had her shoes back on, she stood up, and I finally looked up at her, making eye contact for the first time since the program had finished.

"Do you want a copy of it?"

I held up my phone to show her the video that Terry had taken. I hadn't had a chance to watch it all yet, but from what I had seen, he'd done a great job of staying with us, exactly as I hoped. It looked amazing.

To my surprise, she shook her head. "You said it was for you, so you keep it. I have to go now, I've got class later. Goodbye, Austin."

Why wouldn't she want it? We didn't have any video of that program, and I knew it meant as much to her as it did to me. I wished I understood anything that was going on in her head. The woman I could once read like a book couldn't be more of a mystery to me at that moment.

"We should talk…" I started to say, but she shook her head again.

"You said I owed you a dance," she reminded me, her voice cold and distant, as if she had left all her emotion out on the ice. "You've had it now. Go back to your life and forget you ever saw me."

She moved to walk past me, but I couldn't let her go like that. A hundred things still needed to be said, so I reached out to take hold of her arm.

"I don't want to forget. After all this time… there are things I never got to tell you. Things I never got to ask."

The flash of pain in her eyes nearly took my breath away before she brought herself under control. Her lips pressed tightly together before she spoke again. "You lost the chance to ask me anything a long time ago. I don't owe you anything else."

Her words hit me harder than if she'd actually struck me.

Although I suspected that she still blamed me, to hear her state it so plainly hurt more than I expected. How could I explain to her why I hadn't given her that ride all those years ago and how sorry I was for everything that the accident had cost her?

"It was… it was just a stupid mistake, Amy."

My voice trembled as I tried to express everything I had held inside for so long.

"I was confused and immature. I never meant for this..."

I couldn't even force the words out. My lungs seemed to have stopped working, and I couldn't catch my breath.

The look she gave me didn't help. Outrage flared in her blue eyes. "A mistake? Maybe you can call it a 'mistake', but it changed my whole life! It took away my whole future."

The pain in those words was almost more than I could bear. I wanted to stay calm for this, but I was quickly losing that battle. Against my will, my face scrunched up as I tried to hold back my tears.

"I know. I would give anything to go back and change it. You can't imagine how many times I've replayed it in my head, wishing I had just made a different choice."

One stupid ride. Fifteen minutes of awkwardness was all I had to give her and everything would have been different. Did she really think I didn't know that? That I hadn't felt guilty about it every single day?

She took a deep breath, her eyes closed. Obviously, she found this conversation as difficult as I did, but she managed to keep it together better. "There's no point getting upset. It's all in the past. I've moved on, and obviously, you have too. I don't want to fight. It's just all of this..."

She gestured to me and the rink, to the program that still lingered there on the ice behind us.

"It brought it back up again."

Just because getting upset wouldn't change anything didn't mean we shouldn't talk about it. Why was she so determined not to hear me out?

"I'm still a fan of yours," she continued, clearly trying to bring the conversation to an end. "I hope you do well in Seattle, and the rest of the season. I hope..."

She trailed off, whatever she had been about to say getting caught in her throat, and no matter how hard she tried, she couldn't force it out.

What did she hope? That I won the Olympic medal she'd never have? Didn't she know that thought pained me almost as much as it hurt her?

Instead of finishing the sentence, she shook her head instead.

"Goodbye, Austin," she repeated, walking away and leaving me all alone in the stands, still in my skates.

For her, the story had come to an end, but I didn't see it that way. From my perspective, we still had a long way to go.

"Goodbye until tomorrow," I whispered back.

Chapter Twelve

~**Amelia**~

In the days after skating with Austin, it felt like a fog descended over my life. I tried to concentrate on my classes and the internship, to go on as I had before, but everything felt colder and emptier somehow. That dance we did, that incredible moment of connection on the ice, reminded me of all I had lost and all I would never have again.

Part of me clung on to the memory, to the feeling of being truly whole again for the first time in years, while the other part of me wished it never happened. It would have been easier without the reminder, easier to pretend that I could be just as happy in the new life I'd tried so hard to build for myself.

Besides the moments on the ice, my mind also returned, over and over, to what Austin said afterward. *It was just a stupid mistake.* Was that really what he thought about ending our partnership? Calling it a 'just' a mistake made it feel inconsequential, an insult to both me and to Grace.

And when he said he replayed it over and over in his head, what exactly did he replay? The way he never came to see me in the hospital? The way I had to find out from our coach that he had left to train with someone else because he couldn't even be bothered to tell me himself?

His words didn't make sense to me and neither did the emotion behind them. Deep-rooted hurt tugged on each word, as if he'd somehow suffered as much as I had, and I couldn't understand it.

In the end, though, it didn't matter. I meant what I said: whatever the point of that whole session on the ice had been, we could never go back. What was done was done, and we could only move forward, him with his life and me with mine.

The following weekend, Gaby, Rosa and Jenna gathered in my dorm room as we worked on assignments for school. On my laptop, the online feed from Skate America played silently, the sound muted as I waited for Austin and Grace to take the ice for their rhythm dance.

"Are you sure you want to watch that?" Gaby asked, glancing over at my screen.

I'd filled them all in on the mess with Austin. Gaby agreed with me that it would be best if we weren't in touch any more. Rosa was convinced that he was in love with me, naturally, and Jenna's interest had drifted to watching all the male dancers in their tight pants.

"It's for the profile," I explained to Gaby, sticking to a half-truth. "Since I wrote about his training the week before this event, I should also include how they did."

"You could always look up the results afterwards," Jenna pointed out.

"I could, but I never got to see their full dances either. I only saw bits and pieces that they were working on. I'm curious. That's all."

Even though I could tell they didn't buy my story, they didn't argue any further.

We kept working and chatting until Austin and Grace's turn arrived. While I turned up the sound on the laptop, my friends drew closer to watch it with me.

Their rhythm dance was pretty good. The theme that year was a Latin rhythm, which Austin had always been good at. That hadn't changed. He looked natural and in control as they flew around the ice, each step confident and meaningful. Although I had to admit that I watched him a lot more than I watched Grace, she seemed to do well too.

At the circular step sequence, I smiled to myself when I saw that they incorporated my suggestion for the timing, and that smile grew even wider when it was graded a Level 4. If they hadn't changed it, it would have been a Level 3 instead, I felt certain, which would have affected their overall marks.

In spite of everything, it gave me some satisfaction to know I had helped.

After taking their bows, they skated over to the kiss 'n' cry area, putting their skate guards on and taking a seat.

"Why do they call it the 'kiss 'n' cry'?" Jenna asked from behind me, almost making me jump. I'd forgotten anyone else was in the room.

"It's where the skaters wait for their marks. If they're good marks and they're happy, there will be kisses, and if not, there's crying. It sounds a bit silly, but it's actually a very accurate description."

I'd certainly experienced both sides before.

Austin's arm slid around Grace's shoulders as they waited for their marks, and anybody watching would have believed they were a couple. I pushed down the memory of the way that arm felt around me while I watched their marks come in. Their score put them in second place after the rhythm dance, behind the previous year's world champions.

They couldn't have asked for a much better result. If they could hold onto that position for the free dance the next day, it would set them up well for the rest of the season.

I reached my hand out to turn the sound back down on my laptop, but just before the camera moved off them, Austin looked straight into the camera and mouthed something that looked a lot like, "Thanks, Amy."

My hand froze in mid-air.

I must have imagined it, my mind playing tricks on me after all the heightened emotions of the past couple of weeks. However, one quick glance over at my friends after I turned the sound off told me they had seen it too.

"He just thanked you on national TV!" Rosa squealed.

I shook my head, fighting against the evidence of my own eyes. "It must be some other Amy. That's not even my name anymore."

I hadn't told them about him calling me 'his' Amy since I still didn't know how to even process that myself.

None of them look convinced by my explanation. "I think you got in his head," Jenna suggested. "He's probably been thinking about you every day."

"I really don't think..." I started to say, but my phone buzzed before I could finish. Relieved for the distraction, I snatched it up off my desk, only for that relief to fizzle away.

The text came from Austin.

> *Were you watching?*

Against my will, I glanced back at the screen, but the competition had moved on, another couple now on the ice.

He must have sent it before he even got his skates off, making my attempts to convince myself that he hadn't been thinking about me right after his performance seem futile.

What did it mean? He hadn't been in touch at all since that morning in the rink, and I had assumed he intended to take my advice and forget that he saw me. But if that were the case, why message me now?

I stared at the phone a second too long and Rosa grabbed it out of my hand. Her eyes went almost comically wide as she read the message.

"Oh my God, Mia! I knew it. He wants you."

Rolling my eyes, I took the phone back. "He probably just wanted to know if I saw that they used the change I suggested."

Her eyes rolled even harder. "Not likely. You said he was all over you before he realized who you were."

"Because he felt like he knew me. Which he did, sort of. Since he figured out who I am, he certainly hasn't said anything about asking me out again."

Jenna stepped in curiously. "Would you go, though, if he did ask again?"

"He won't," I assured her.

She gave me a sly grin. "That doesn't answer my question. You should probably think about it. You know I don't always agree with Rosa's take on things, but in this case, I think she's got a point. He's clearly thinking about you."

Gaby hadn't said anything, keeping uncharacteristically quiet, and when I glanced over at her to see why, concern lined the edges of her tight lips. Among the four of us, we'd been friends the longest, and she understood the most about how hard it had been for me to get over losing my dreams. In her eyes, I could see the fear of me getting hurt again, and it was a fear I shared. It was the reason I pushed Austin away after skating with him the other day.

Seeing me looking at her, she tried to smile. "Are you going to text him back?"

"Yeah," I said, trying to make it sound like no big deal. "I'm still writing the article. I'll tell him that I saw it, and that's it."

Looking down at my phone, I composed a reply.

> I watched. Great skate.

After hitting send, I showed it to them. The tightness in Gaby's face relaxed while Rosa groaned. "You need to give him a little more than that. He's going to think you don't care at all."

Ready to move on from this whole conversation, I put my phone back down, but a few seconds later it buzzed again and I couldn't stop myself from checking to see what it said.

> *Level 4 on step sequence – thanks to you.*

A smile flashed across my face at the simple words. Of course Austin would give me credit for that. He'd always been quick to appreciate my contributions on the ice, believing in me and encouraging me to speak my mind more than anyone else ever had.

The smile faded, though, as I remembered how that made it hurt even more when he moved on so quickly rather than waiting for me to recover. Whatever he felt for my talents on the ice, it obviously hadn't been enough.

Putting the phone back down again, I left the text on read. Nothing else needed to be said. With the profile done, we had no reason to keep in touch anymore, and the best plan of action would be to move on and leave all of this in the past, where it belonged.

~Austin~

Getting changed in the locker room after our rhythm dance, the smile seemed stuck on my face. We skated well. The first time we performed a new dance in front of an audience, we could never be sure how it would go over, but both the audience and the judges responded to it well. Our marks were only slightly behind the team that would be our biggest competition that year.

Those were all good reasons to be smiling, but none of them fully explained the grin I couldn't seem to shake. It had a lot more to do with the fact that Amy had been watching.

Before her reply to my text, I hadn't heard from her since the morning we skated together. I tried to give her time and space to make the next move. She said that seeing me and skating with me stirred up a lot of emotions for her, which I completely understood since it stirred up a lot of things for me too. But now that I knew she lived in the same city as me, that she was so close to me at any given time, I couldn't get her out of my mind.

There had to be a reason we'd been brought together again and I didn't intend to ignore that.

So, when she still hadn't reached out to me by the time we got to Seattle, I tested the waters by messaging her to ask if she watched our skate. The fact that she did struck me as a very good sign.

I also couldn't stop thinking about the program, the one we skated together and Terry filmed for me. I'd watched the video dozens of times already, and the program was even better than I remembered it. Honestly, it was miles ahead of the free dance that Grace and I would be debuting the next day. If we had a dance like The Last 5 Years instead, one suited to us the way that one was made just for Amy and me, our chances of success would be so much better.

Every time it crossed my mind, I had to bite my tongue to keep from mentioning it to our coach and telling him how I'd rather be doing a program like that. If I hadn't promised Amy to keep it quiet, I would have already shown him. She seemed so upset at the thought of me using any of it with Grace, but on the other hand, it didn't seem right for her brilliance to remain unseen either.

I'd always known what a talented choreographer Amy was, and I wanted everyone else to know it too.

The next afternoon, Grace and I travelled together from our hotel to the rink for the free dance, going through our usual routines. Although I didn't consider myself superstitious, necessarily, I'd found what worked for me before a competition and I liked to stick to it. That included not looking at my phone before we went on since I needed to keep my head in the game and stay focused on the job we had to do.

That afternoon, I couldn't help it. I checked more than once, hoping for a text from Amy, some words of encouragement or anything to let me know that she would be watching again. It never came, but I couldn't shake the feeling that she would be watching anyway, and it made me want to perform better than ever.

Grace and I went out for our warm-up before the dance, taking the ice with the other three couples in the final group. With Seattle so close to the Canadian border, we had a big Canadian cheering section, and it almost felt like there were more Canadian fans in the arena than there were Americans. I always looked around the crowd a bit during the warm-up, taking note of any particularly colourful signs or anything else that might distract me during our actual program. If I knew where they all were beforehand, it would help me ignore them later.

"Everything okay?" Grace asked as she took my hand in the centre of the ice to begin our joint warm-up. She always asked me that; another part of our routine.

"Good. You?"

I always checked in with her too, making sure nothing was bothering her that might affect our performance. She nodded back at me, but I could tell neither of us was being entirely truthful. She looked nervous, and I felt it too. We both lacked the confidence in our free dance that we had about the rhythm dance we'd done the day before. Too much of it still felt unready, but at that point, all we could do was skate it as well as possible and hope for the best.

When the warm-up finished, we headed back off the ice, sliding our guards onto our blades and returning to the locker rooms. We were the last team to skate that afternoon. A random draw decided the skating order within each group, so the team that led the competition, the previous year's world champions from France, were skating first, followed by the teams in the third and fourth places, and finally us.

I paced the hall outside the locker rooms, trying to keep my muscles loose and warm, while Grace ran through elements of the dance at the opposite end of the hall. We never spoke to each other during this part of the competition, not wanting to say the wrong thing and get in each other's head.

At last, our turn came and we headed back out to the ice.

The applause for the team that had just finished echoed around the arena and they looked pleased as they came off the ice. I never paid attention to the other team's marks when we skated since they were completely outside of my control. All I could control was our own performance and what happened when we went out there.

We did another short warm-up, separate from each other, while the other team's marks were announced, and finally, we could begin. We took our starting positions and the opening strains of the music floated into the arena, filling the air around us. My world narrowed until only Grace and the ice remained. All I could hear was the music. The crowd disappeared, the judges vanished, and all that mattered was the dance.

The first element out of the gate was the lift that Mia... or Amy, rather... helped us fix. It went well, the new entrance working much better for us.

That turned out to be the highlight of the whole program. After the lift, things started to go wrong.

We carried a lot of speed into the straight-line step sequence, but by the end, we were struggling to hit the beats of the music. All our momentum had been lost. Our hands slipped against each other when they should have been secure.

Worst of all, coming out of a spin, an element that shouldn't have caused us any trouble at all, Grace caught a bad edge and fell. It took us several seconds to catch back up to the music and we gave up trying to perform the interpretation, focusing on making it through with no more major mistakes instead.

Polite applause came from the crowd when we finished, but we both knew it had been nowhere near good enough, and nowhere near where we needed to be for an Olympic year.

"Sorry," Grace whispered to me as I gave her a hug before we took our bows. I shook my head, trying to tell her without words that I didn't blame her. Everyone fell sometimes, and even without the fall, the dance just didn't work. I had suspected as much in practice, and after that disaster of a performance, I knew for sure. We needed to make some drastic changes, and soon.

By the time we sat down in the kiss 'n' cry, Grace's eyes were growing red so I quickly put my arm around her and pulled her close to me. "It's not a big deal," I whispered in her ear. "First competition of the year is all about getting the kinks out, right? It'll get better."

I wished I felt as confident of that as I sounded.

When our marks came up, they were bad, at least by our standards. The judges placed us fourth in the free dance and third overall. The team that came second had been tenth at the previous year's Worlds, where we were second.

That was not the start to the season that we wanted, to say the least.

Obviously, we weren't the only ones who felt that way. By the time we got back to the hotel restaurant for dinner, my mom was on the warpath.

"They were downgraded on two elements!" she yelled at our coach. "What are we paying you for if you can't even figure out what levels they're going to get?"

Having plenty of experience with my mother, Brian responded with admirable stoicism. "On the step sequence, an error forced the downgrading, and for the lift, the judge disagreed with the choreographer's interpretation of the edge change. These things can be fixed, Cynthia. We've got a long time between now and February."

As they continued to argue back and forth, Grace sank down further into her seat, looking like she wanted to disappear, but she really didn't have anything to worry about. My mom never tore into *her*, even when she messed up like she had that day. She never went after Grace the way she used to criticize Amy. If Amy had fallen that way in a major competition, I didn't even want to think about what my mom would have said.

"The problem is the program," I finally cut in, silencing everyone. "We don't like it."

A moment of silence followed my declaration and I understood their surprise. Usually, I limited my contributions to the post-competition analysis to commenting on the performance. Very rarely did Grace or I talk about the programs themselves.

"It needs some tweaks," my mom started to say, but I shook my head, cutting her off.

"No. Tweaks won't be enough. We need a program that we really believe in for this year, and this isn't it. Either we start over or we go back to an old program, because I don't want to perform this one again."

The stunned look in my mom's eyes almost made me smile. I never stood up to her that way, and I couldn't be entirely sure what made me do it then. I could only guess that it had something to do with seeing Amy again. Maybe she reminded me of how she used to fight to improve our programs. Maybe doing her program again with her reminded me how good it felt to skate a program I believed in.

Whatever the reason, I knew that our program that year wouldn't be good enough, and if I didn't say something, we were going to be stuck with it.

"I don't know if Armand will be willing to start from scratch," Brian warned, but that didn't worry me. Working on a new program with the choreographer my mom brought in was the last thing I wanted to do since he obviously didn't understand us at all.

"That's not what I had in mind."

Taking a deep breath, I fished my phone out of my pocket and pulled up the video of me and Amy.

I'd promised her I wouldn't show it to anyone, but I was running out of options. Would she hate me for it? Maybe, but would that really be such a change? She'd already told me she didn't think we should be in each other's lives anymore.

At the end of the day, her talent deserved to be seen, and maybe this would be the way to do it. Breaking my promise was a risk, but if it meant even a chance of getting her on our team, it felt worth it to take the shot.

"Here. Take a look at this."

~Amelia~

The Monday afternoon after Skate America, I sat at my desk in the Urban Style office, finishing off my draft for Austin's profile. After watching their free dance the day before, it didn't surprise me not to hear from Austin again afterwards. Even aside from the way they performed it, the dance didn't work. Perhaps that was a harsh assessment, but true all the same.

For another dance team, it might have been okay, but for Austin and Grace, it looked forced and uncomfortable. It felt like the choreographer hadn't taken the time to get to know them and their strengths before designing it, as if he pulled something off the shelf and expected it to work for them. They were going to have to do a lot of work on it if they wanted to have any chance for the rest of the season. Austin probably had his hands full dealing with all of that, making him too busy to message me.

Not that I cared, I reminded myself. My article had me busy too. Because I jumped on the idea and arranged the interviews so quickly, it would actually be the first article in the new athletic series to be published, and the idea of seeing it in print with my first real byline, not counting the university's newspaper, gave me a little buzz of excitement. Not quite like the rush of performing in front of a crowd, maybe, but it would still be a great addition to my portfolio.

Journalism was the life I wanted now. Why did I have to keep reminding myself of that?

"Hey, Mia, do you have a minute? I've got the photos for your article." Paul appeared beside my desk with a folder in his hands, and I smiled up at him gratefully. The pictures were the last element I needed, and I couldn't wait to see what he'd captured.

"Perfect timing. Please, sit down."

He grabbed a chair and pulled it up next to me, placing the folder on the desk in front of us. His chair felt a little closer than it strictly needed to be, making me remember how both Austin and Grace thought something might be going on between Paul and me. Maybe they saw something that I missed?

Would that be such a bad thing? Paul was a nice guy. I'd never thought of him that way before, but maybe I should have, especially since I had no other dating prospects at the moment.

After twenty minutes reviewing the photos and deciding which ones we liked best for the feature, Paul pulled out another, smaller folder from the back of the file and flipped it open. "These are the ones I took of you. You can keep them if you'd like."

My breath caught in my throat as I flipped through the photos of me and Austin together, dancing the Paso Doble. Even though I knew how good it felt at the time, to see it from the outside, to see our matching lines and placements, drove home one more time how good we had been together... and how we would never be that way again.

On top of that, the way Austin looked at me in the photos made my heart trip over itself. While we danced, I'd done my best to avoid looking at him, but in every picture, he watched me with a look on his face that I could only describe as admiration.

Perhaps even more than that.

But that all happened before he knew the woman in front of him was me, I had to remind myself, flipping the folder closed before I could get even more emotional. What was wrong with me? I thought I buried all those feelings a long time ago, but seeing Austin and being back on the ice with him had disturbed the peace I'd manufactured for myself and I didn't seem to be able to put it to rest again, no matter how hard I tried.

I did my best to smile at Paul in a way that concealed all of my inner turmoil. "Thank you for these. They're beautiful."

That was an understatement. Paul had true talent with his camera, and I tried to turn the conversation in that direction to give me a chance to collect myself.

"I'd never be able to take photos like this. I never seem to get the lighting or the angle right."

"I bet you could learn," he encouraged me. "Not everyone's a natural at it, but a lot of it can be taught. I'd be happy to show you a few tricks sometime."

Not only did that sound interesting, it might actually help me with some of my assignments to be able to take better photos on my own. "I would love that."

"How about this weekend? We could go down to the waterfront, try a few things, and go for lunch?"

It almost sounded like a date, but since he didn't call it that, I didn't want to assume anything. "Sounds good. Here, let me give you my number and you can let me know where to meet you."

He handed me his phone so I could put it in, and I gasped when I saw the time. *Damn it.* I was going to be late for class. Quickly, I input my number and packed up my things, said goodbye to everyone in the office and ran back towards campus.

My phone rang along the way and, suspecting it must have been one of my friends wondering where I was, I pulled it out and answered without checking the call display. "Hello?"

"Hi, is this Amy Gardiner?" a man on the other end asked, and my whole body immediately tensed.

No one who knew me by that name had my number, other than Austin, and the voice definitely didn't belong to him.

"No, sorry, you must have the wrong number."

I hung up before he could say anything else and shoved the phone back in my pocket. A minute later, it rang again, but with my classroom just ahead of me, I ignored it. It went to voicemail just as I sneaked into the back of the room and grabbed a seat, thankfully avoiding the professor's notice.

After class, I made a quick stop back at my dorm to drop off my bag and headed to the cafeteria, where Gaby and Jenna were already waiting. Rosa had an evening class so she wouldn't be joining us that evening. As usual, we chatted about the day and our assignments over dinner until Jenna asked me about something on my schedule and I pulled out my phone to check my calendar.

The voicemail alert on my home screen reminded me of the earlier phone call, which I'd completely put out of my mind. Apologizing to my friends, I dialed in and listened to the message to satisfy my curiosity.

"Hi, this is Brian Sills, calling for Mia Wilson. I'm sorry, I guess I used the wrong name for you earlier. I'm Austin Black and Grace Matthews' coach. We met a couple of weeks ago but we weren't properly introduced."

My heart rate increased with every word. Of course I remembered him, but why would Austin's coach be calling me?

"Austin showed me the video of the program that you created, and we're interested in getting your input into this year's free dance. We would compensate you for your time, naturally. If you have some availability, please give me a call back and we can set up a time for you to come in and discuss it. Thanks."

The message ended, but I didn't move, the phone still held up to my ear as I tried to make sense of everything he just said.

One thing stood out above all others.

Austin showed me the video.

He promised me he wouldn't. He said it would be just for him, and I had been stupid enough to believe that he meant it.

My fingers shaking with growing rage, I called Austin's number.

He answered on the second ring. "Amy, I'm sorry."

Not even a hello. Obviously, he knew the reason for my call. He knew what he'd done.

"You said you wouldn't show it to anyone." My voice trembled in anger, despite my best attempts to keep it steady.

"I know. I didn't plan to, but we were talking about the kind of program we needed, and it was so much easier to show them than try to explain it. But you're right, I still shouldn't have done it. It was a dick move and I'm sorry."

He did sound apologetic, but I wasn't in a forgiving mood. "Why didn't you tell me?" I demanded. His coach wouldn't have reached out with Austin's approval. He wouldn't have had my number if Austin hadn't given it to him, so why didn't he warn me?

"I thought you might not be so upset if you heard it from someone else," he admitted sheepishly. "And I thought it might soften the blow a bit if you heard the rest of the offer too."

"You're not using that program," I told him, repeating what I had already said back on the ice, before we skated it. "I don't know how it works, but I must have some kind of rights…"

"Amy, I don't want to use that program," he interrupted. "Not any of it. That's not what this is about. We want you to create something entirely new."

In my anger, I hadn't even really absorbed the rest of his coach's message. What exactly did he say? Something about getting my input?

"I know you could come up with something amazing," Austin continued. "And as great as it would be for us, it could be really great for you too. Everyone will finally see what you can do."

Something in his tone made me pause, made me bite back the words of dismissal that lingered on the tip of my tongue. The sincerity in his words felt comfortingly familiar, the same sincerity he'd always had when encouraging me on the ice.

Still, he'd broken his word. He made the decision for both of us, just like before.

I stayed quiet for so long that Austin spoke again before I replied.

"I get why you're angry, I really do, and I know that 'sorry' doesn't fix it. But please, don't turn this down just because of me. We don't have to be friends or even talk off the ice, if that's what you want, but I trust you, Amy. I know that if you agree to this, you'll give us the best program we've ever had, and we'll all benefit from it. Every skater will want to work with you once they see it. Don't make any decisions right away, okay? Think about it for a while. Please."

He sounded almost desperate, and I wondered if, somehow, this was his way of trying to make amends. Maybe he thought that offering me this opportunity would be a way of making it up to me for abandoning me all those years ago?

I supposed I could think it over. There was no harm in that, but I didn't need to discuss it any further with him. It would be something I needed to decide for myself.

"I'll think about it," I agreed, hanging up before he could say anything else.

As soon as I put the phone down, the full implications of the offer started to take shape in my head, and a new feeling bubbled up inside me, one I hadn't felt in a long time.

Purpose.

It could actually be an incredible opportunity. When I did the profile on Austin, it felt so fulfilling to make suggestions that made their dances better. And ever since Austin and I skated our program together, the program I created, my brain had been full of new ideas, new moves and new steps, and I had nowhere to put them.

Out of nowhere, I was being offered the chance to work on a program that would be skated by some of the best dancers in the world, in front of an international audience at the Olympics.

Austin was right: if people liked what I came up with, it could lead to more offers. It could mean really big things for me, and possibly even a whole new career.

However, it would also mean working with Austin and Grace, seeing them skating together and dealing with all the other feelings that Austin brought up in me.

Did I really want a daily reminder of what I had lost? I'd worked so hard to move on and build a new dream for myself, but despite the accomplishment I felt at getting my article printed, I knew deep in my heart that it didn't compare to the passion I had for skating.

Would this be a step forwards or a step back?

Belatedly, I realized that Gaby and Jenna had both stopped talking. I'd almost forgotten they were there, but they must have heard at least my side of the conversation with Austin because when I looked up at them, they both stared at me curiously.

"What's going on?" Gaby asked.

"Is everything okay?" Jenna added.

"I'm not really sure," I admitted, looking down at the phone in my hand again as if it would give me the answer as to what I should do next. "But I think it's going to be."

Chapter Thirteen

~Austin~

Standing outside my mom's house, I paused for a second before knocking, feeling strange to be there as a visitor. I moved out the previous year, deciding the expense of having a place of my own would be worth the independence it gave me, and I hadn't been back to visit since. That didn't mean I didn't see her. She spent most days at the rink, making it unnecessary for me to come to her house.

That day, however, we needed to talk.

Ever since I showed everyone in Seattle the video of Amy and me dancing, she'd been fuming. She didn't approve of me seeing Amy at all, and definitely didn't agree with asking her to work with us even though I knew in my heart it would be the best thing for Grace and me.

We needed a program that worked for us. For that, we needed Amy, which meant convincing my mom to back off.

I'd never had much luck doing that before, but I'd never been quite so motivated either.

"Austin? Is everything okay?"

My mom's features formed a perfect picture of surprise when I finally knocked and she opened the door. It was a sad commentary on our relationship that visiting her suggested something might be wrong, but that didn't make it less true.

"I have to talk to you about a few things. Let's go sit down."

After following her into the house, I sat across from her in the living room, looking around with a new perspective after my long absence. The room could have passed as a shrine. Pictures of me dotted the walls and filled frames on the side tables and bookshelves. My first time on the ice. My first competition, my first medal. My first front-page newspaper photo.

Had it always been like this? I didn't remember it being quite so intense, but it certainly felt uncomfortable now.

It made what I'd come there to tell her even harder, but I forced myself to dive right in. No matter how I approached it, she wasn't going to like it.

"There's not really an easy way to say this, but I think you should take a break from managing me. Take a holiday or something. Take some time for yourself."

If I hoped that framing it as a reward for her would help, it didn't. Her eyes went wide in surprise, staring at me as though I just suggested she take a one-way trip to the moon. "What do you mean? You need me."

Keeping my tone as calm as I could, I went a little deeper. "You've helped me a lot, but the surprise media appearances? Not helpful. And I know about the off-limit list. What's the point of that? You know I never asked for anything like that."

She didn't know I knew about the list, and it obviously caught her off guard, but just like she always did, she immediately tried to rationalize it.

"I don't want to bother you for every little thing. I'm just looking out for you so you can focus on your skating and not worry about everything else."

"But I do worry," I tried to explain. "I worry because I don't know what else you're doing without telling me. If you really wanted to help me, you'd keep me in the loop about these things. It's worse to be left wondering exactly what you're doing on my behalf."

"Austin, it's really nothing for you to concern yourself with," she said in what I assumed was meant to be a soothing tone. "It's all under control."

"Under your control, you mean," I shot back. Bitterness seeped into the words, despite my best efforts, and her face tightened at my tone.

"Where is this coming from? It never bothered you before." Before I could answer the question, her brow cleared when she reached her own conclusion. "This is about Amy, isn't it?"

The day my mom told me Amy didn't want to skate with me again was the last time we really discussed my former partner. My mom preferred to pretend she never existed and since the whole subject remained a sore spot for me, I didn't bring her up either. However, as with everything else I came there to say that day, the time seemed to have come to clear the air on that subject too.

"It's not directly about Amy, but since you brought her up, you should know that Brian has been in touch with her. He's asked her to work on the free dance with us."

My mom's jaw clenched, her nostrils flaring in defiance. "There are hundreds of qualified choreographers out there who can..."

"No," I cut her off, not letting her get started. "I want Amy. I want to do the program that she can create for us."

She tried a different tack. "You've always thought too highly of that girl."

"And you never gave her enough credit," I countered. "The program she created for us was amazing. You want us to win, right? This is our best chance."

"And what about everything that happened between you? How she blamed you for the accident? That's not going to be a distraction?"

My chest tightened as it always did at the reminder of the part I'd played in Amy's injuries.

"Have you talked about it?" she asked.

"We haven't," I admitted. "She doesn't want to talk about it, but it doesn't matter because this isn't about us. It has nothing to do with our past. This is about getting the best program now, for me and for Grace, and if you think Amy's going to be petty and not bring her best for us, you really don't know her at all."

"So, she hasn't said anything about what happened?" my mom pressed, still stuck on that part of the conversation.

Something in the question made me pause. Aside from the usual contempt in her voice whenever she spoke about Amy, I could detect a different emotion too, something that felt closer to anxiety. As if she were worried about something Amy could have said.

I watched her reaction carefully as I answered. "No, she hasn't. Why? Is there something I should know?"

My mom's lips pursed, confirming my suspicions: there was something she wasn't telling me.

My jaw set firmly as I tried to brace myself for whatever it might be. "What don't I know, Mom?"

Glancing away from me, she swallowed, the muscles in her throat working to force the motion. As I took in how nervous she seemed, I started to get nervous too. Whatever she had to tell me, it felt significant.

Finally, she looked back at me, straightening her shoulders as if steeling herself for my reaction. "Do you remember, after the accident, when I told you that Karen said Amy wasn't coming back? When we decided to move to Toronto with Grace?"

Of course I remembered. What kind of a ridiculous question was that?

I simply nodded, waiting for her to get to the point.

"Well..." She grimaced, pausing one more time before pushing the words out. "That might not have been exactly what happened."

"What do you mean 'not exactly what happened'? Exactly what *did* happen?"

Her arms crossed over her chest as if they could provide some defense against my response. "It had been months. *Months*, Austin, and we hadn't heard anything from the Gardiners. You needed to move on."

My heart began to thud, my stomach twisting as I started to get an idea where this was heading.

The question came out just above a whisper. "What did you do?"

"I did what had to be done. You and Grace were working well together, so there was no need to wait around any longer. I told Karen we were done."

"Done?" I echoed, hoping desperately that I'd misinterpreted what she meant.

I hadn't.

"I told her we were leaving and your partnership with Amy was finished."

A new fissure of grief opened up inside me, joining the others that already existed in the part of my heart that belonged to Amy. "*You* ended it?"

"I did what had to be done, what was best for you," she repeated stubbornly. "I've only ever wanted the best for you, Austin."

"And breaking my partnership with the best dancer I've ever met was 'best' for me?"

She couldn't possibly believe that, but she argued with me anyway. "You've done well with Grace. It hasn't hurt you."

Maybe not in skating terms, but personally? It hurt me a hell of a lot, and more than that, it hurt Amy.

Suddenly, the things she said to me when I asked about her abandoned skating career made a lot more sense.

It's hard to dance without a partner.

Oh, God. My stomach twisted again, almost making me feel sick. She thought *I* didn't want to skate with her anymore, while I always thought it had been the other way around.

When I didn't say anything, too stunned by her revelation to form a coherent sentence, my mom added one more thing. "It's no different from what you did to Grace when you left her for Amy in the first place."

Those words hit me like a slap in the face and I stared at my mother as if seeing her for the very first time. "You did this on purpose? So I would skate with Grace again?"

"Did what, Austin?" Her apologetic, nervous tone vanished and she transitioned to full offense. "I didn't cause Amy's accident and I didn't force her to stay away from you all those months. I just did what was best based on the situation we were in. Maybe she would have come back eventually and maybe she wouldn't have, but you'd waited long enough."

"That wasn't your call," I whispered, almost choking on the words. "I would have waited as long as it took."

My mom's lips formed a thin line. "Exactly, and that's why I had to make the call for you. When you've got that Olympic medal around your neck, you'll see I was right."

I had no more words. If she couldn't see what she'd done wrong, even after all this time, I didn't know how I'd ever make her understand.

"Don't come back to the rink until I'm ready to see you again. You're officially on leave."

"Austin..."

She tried to call out after me but I didn't stop, heading out the door before she could twist the situation any more than she already had.

IT FIGURES

~Amelia~

The following day, the phone call from Austin's coach dominated my thoughts even as I tried to focus on my classes and the other demands of my life. I hadn't returned his call yet since I didn't know what to do. Could I put my past behind me and seize this opportunity, or would I be recklessly slicing open old wounds that took years to heal in the first place?

Very few people could understand the depth of my dilemma, but one person could come close to it, so in the early evening, I gave her a call.

"Hi, Mia." My mom's enthusiastic greeting lifted my spirits, as usual. "I've missed you. How are you?"

Other than a few texts, I hadn't spoken to my mother for two weeks, not since I asked her for Austin's mom's phone number. I kept the information I shared about my interviews with Austin to the bare minimum, and I certainly hadn't told her that he discovered my subterfuge. Telling her everything wouldn't be easy, but I needed to get her on the same page if I wanted her advice on what to do next.

"I'm good, but I need to talk to you about Austin."

Instantly, her tone cooled several degrees. "What about him?"

Sharing only the necessary details, I explained to her that Austin knew who I was, that we'd skated together, and that his coach wanted my help.

A long moment of silence followed my explanation before she finally spoke. "I feel like you're leaving quite a lot out."

"Maybe a little, but that's the gist of it."

I really didn't want to go into my mixed-up feelings about Austin himself, not when she never knew exactly how I felt about him in the first place. My long-standing crush had been a closely-guarded secret, even after he was no longer in my life.

"Have you talked to him about the accident?"

She sounded worried, as if she feared what it would do to my emotional state to revisit that time in my life, so I sought to reassure her. "No, and there's no need to. This isn't about the past or about us at all.

I've moved on and I told him so. If I help them with their program, it would be strictly professional."

Another long silence followed, and I could tell she was struggling. For the past four years, my mom had done her best to pretend Austin never existed. Ever since we found out he left to partner with Grace, he'd been dead to her.

"I don't have any illusions about skating with Austin again, if that's what you're worried about," I added when she still didn't say anything. "We all know that ship sailed a long time ago, but I like the creative side of things and a lot of people would see the program. It's a great opportunity and it might lead to other opportunities too."

Finally, she spoke again. "I thought you were happy with university and the internship. Isn't writing what you want to do now?"

"I *am* happy. It's not like I'm giving up on school or anything, but being back on the ice with Austin reminded me of just how much I loved creating our program. This wouldn't take up that much time. It might not even turn into anything at all, but I feel like I should at least try."

Before our conversation, I hadn't felt quite so certain, but in the course of convincing her, things were becoming clearer to me too.

"You know I think you're brilliant, and I know you could create a beautiful program. But do you really want to do it for Austin and Grace? Why them, of all people? You could work with someone else instead."

"Nobody else has asked me," I countered. "How else am I going to get a chance to do it at this level right away, with no other experience? This program would be performed at the Olympics! The whole world would see it."

She sighed, knowing I had a point. "It kind of sounds to me like you've already made up your mind. I just… I don't know, Mia. What if this just pulls you right back to where you were when we got the news from Karen? I don't want you to have to go through anything like that again."

A lump filled my throat at the reminder of that day, but I did my best to swallow it down. "Nothing like that is going to happen."

When she sighed, I could hear the resignation in it. "If that's what you want, then of course I support you. Just be careful, sweetheart."

"I will," I promised, and after we hung up, I sat there for a few more minutes, reviewing everything my mom said and the things Austin had said to me too.

We didn't have to be friends. We didn't have to talk about the past, and maybe it would be best if we didn't. Although it hadn't been easy, I'd made my peace with the path my life took, and I wouldn't let it bring me down again.

~Three years earlier~

The posters on the walls of the doctor's office in St John's were so familiar to me, I could have recited several of them off by heart. For the past six months, I met with the doctor regularly, along with my intensive physiotherapy and rehab, making sure everything stayed on track for a full recovery.

At my last appointment, he said that if everything looked good in my next x-rays, he would sign off on me getting back on the ice, and I couldn't wait.

Getting back on the ice meant going home. Back to Ottawa and the club there. Back to my dad, who'd stayed behind for work. Back to Austin.

Back to my life.

The thought of it made me happier than I could express, but nerves fluttered around the edge of my excitement. In those six months, I hadn't heard a single word from Austin. Every time I mentioned wanting to speak to him, my mom would say that I should focus on getting better without any distractions. Although I couldn't help feeling she wasn't telling me the whole story, I also couldn't deny she had a point. My rehab took up all my time, and with my singular focus, I'd exceeded every goal my therapists set.

Hopefully, all my hard work was about to pay off. If the doctor gave me the green light that day, my mom had promised she'd call Karen and Austin's mom to give them the good news, and if Austin was there, she'd let me talk to him too.

The doctor bustled into the room with a folder in his hand and a smile on his face. "Hello, Amy. How are you feeling?"

"Really good." I kept my answer simple since we reviewed my condition regularly. The pain had disappeared unless I pushed to the edges of my flexibility. I'd started working out again, not as intensely as before, but enough that my stamina was starting to return, and it would only get better from there. I would keep working as hard as I had to, as long as I needed to.

He sat down next to me and opened the folder on his desk, displaying the black-and-white images within. "Your x-rays look great," he confirmed. "The bones have completely mended, good as new."

A wide smile broke out on my face. "Can I start skating again?"

When he nodded, I practically bounced in my seat, giddy with relief and excitement.

"Of course you'll need to ease yourself back in. Don't push yourself too hard. But I know you've been taking this all seriously and following orders, so just keep doing that and you'll be fine."

As we walked out of the clinic, not even the blustery March wind could bring down my spirits. "When can we fly home?" I asked my mom, ready to leave immediately if she said the word. I couldn't wait to get back.

"I'll give Karen a call and see what she says. It might take a bit of time to sort everything out."

Despite the smile she gave me, her level of enthusiasm seemed significantly lower than mine, but I chalked it up to the fact that she really enjoyed living in St John's and would probably miss it when we left.

Moving to Newfoundland had been her idea. Her sister, my aunt, worked at a private physiotherapy clinic on the island, and my mom thought no one would be more dedicated to my recovery than family. It also gave us both a change of pace and scenery, removing me from anything that might trigger depression over the accident and making it into something of an adventure instead.

Since my dad couldn't leave his job, he returned to Ottawa after driving us out. He called me regularly, though he and my mom didn't seem to talk too much. My mom hadn't said anything to me, but I had my suspicions that the separation hadn't helped their marriage. The sooner we went back, the better it would be for everyone, at least from my point of view.

When we got back to my aunt's house, my mom sent me down to the basement to run through my rehab exercises while she started making phone calls and plans. Buzzing with energy, I had to keep myself from overdoing it, but when my mom came down the stairs fifteen minutes later, her steps heavy and slow, I knew immediately that something had to be wrong.

"What's going on?" I asked tentatively as she sank down onto the sofa pushed against one wall of the room. We'd cleared as much space as possible in the centre of the room for my rehab, and I stayed where I was on the floor, stretching out my injured leg.

She didn't immediately answer me, and the dread in my chest squeezed tighter. The pallor of her face reminded me of the day I woke up in the hospital, and worst-case scenarios raced through my head with alarming speed. Did someone else get hurt? Did someone die? Why didn't she just tell me?

"I'm so sorry, honey," she whispered, those words doing nothing to calm my nerves.

"Sorry about what?"

She didn't answer me directly, saying instead, "I talked to Karen."

"And?" I asked, still not having a clue where this was going.

"Austin's no longer at the club."

At first, I didn't understand what she was saying. "You mean he left for the day?"

She shook her head, tears gathering in her eyes. "No. He *left*. Permanently."

The room spun around me, and I reached for the ground beneath me to keep my balance. There must have been some mistake. Austin would never quit, not without telling me. We may have been apart for months, but I *knew* him. He loved dancing too much. "Let me talk to him. I'll convince him to come back. He can't quit."

She took a deep breath, squeezing her eyes closed. "He didn't quit. He found a new partner."

The room spun again, and that time, I couldn't stop it.

"He left because he moved to a different club to train with her. He's gone, so there's no reason for us to go back. I'm so sorry, Amy."

Through the tears that suddenly blinded me, I could see my mom crying too. "It's not your fault," I whispered, trying to comfort her even as my own world crashed down around me. I didn't want her to blame herself, not for the accident and not for this.

I could see clearly enough what happened.

Finally, Austin's silence over the long, lonely months of rehab made sense to me. He never got in touch because he never intended for us to skate together again.

Maybe he thought I wouldn't be able to recover. Maybe he blamed me for losing the season, just as I feared he would. My mom had never let me apologize the way I wanted to, and maybe he moved on simply out of resentment.

For months, I pushed myself, working hard every day to get better, all with the goal of returning to him, only to find out I had nothing to go back to. It had all been for nothing, and for the first time since that day in the hospital, I gave in to the grief of not only my lost season but the loss of the only future I ever wanted.

The accident might have caused my injuries, but that day broke my heart.

~Austin~

~Present day~

Back at my house, my mind continued to reel from the bomb my mom dropped on me. All those years, I thought Amy decided to end our partnership. I thought that she'd been so upset with me, with my actions that led to her accident, that she didn't want to skate with me anymore.

Now, I knew that simply wasn't true.

Amy *had* gone missing after the accident, that much still appeared to be right. My mom swore that we didn't hear anything from Amy or her family for months and I believed her, if only because it made no sense to lie about that she already confessed something far worse.

My mom told Karen we were done waiting for Amy to come back, and I could only assume that Karen passed that message on to Amy. From there, I could guess exactly how it would have made her feel, because it would have been the same sense of profound loss I felt when I thought she'd been the one to end things.

It's hard to dance without a partner.

The accusation in those words cut even deeper than before. In her view, I abandoned her in what must have been an incredibly difficult time for her. I left her behind, choosing to skate with someone who didn't have to recover from painful injuries. And apparently, I *did* do those things, even if I didn't know I was doing them and never would have done them on purpose.

If I'd known she wanted to come back, I would have waited for her, as long as it took.

But if she intended to return, why the radio silence? Why didn't she read my texts? Why didn't her mom get in touch with mine to keep us updated on Amy's progress? Why did it feel like she completely vanished off the face of the earth?

Too many things still didn't make sense to me, and they wouldn't make sense until we had a chance to finally sit down and talk about exactly what happened four years ago.

A dozen times, I pulled out my phone to call her, and each time, I stopped myself. We needed to have this conversation face-to-face. I needed to look in her eyes as we hashed it out, and at that moment, I didn't know if she'd even agree to see me. I'd just broken her trust, again, by showing Brian the video of our dance, and I didn't want to interfere with her decision about whether or not to work on our program.

So much was still up in the air, and I didn't want to push her away when we were finally so close to being a team again, even in a different way than before.

I shoved my phone back into my pocket for the thirteenth time right when my doorbell rang, startling me out of my thoughts. I rarely had unexpected visitors, and especially not on a training night. Maybe my mom followed me home? Were there more awful secrets she'd hidden from me?

Ignoring the doorbell was tempting, but in the end, I gave in and went to answer it. My heart sank when I saw the person standing there: not my mom, but not a lot better either, considering my current mood.

"Grace? What's going on?"

She gave me a tight smile, looking almost as uncomfortable as I felt. "I need to talk to you."

Although part of me wanted to ask why she didn't call before coming over, I didn't really have to. I knew why. If she had, I would have told her not to come, so she probably decided she'd have better luck just turning up.

Not wanting to be a jerk and send her away when she'd made the effort to be there, I gave in. "Sure. Come on in."

In my kitchen, I offered her something to drink, and once we both had a mug of herbal tea and took a seat at the kitchen table, she explained the reason for her visit.

"I've been thinking about it, and I'm not sure that I'm comfortable having Amy working with us."

My stomach sank yet again. Apparently, it wasn't enough that my mom and Amy wanted to fight me on this. I had to convince Grace too.

Perhaps I should have expected it. When Grace and I started skating together after Amy's accident, a lot of people made comments comparing her to Amy in a way that didn't flatter Grace. Maybe she feared inviting those comparisons again.

"You know this has nothing to do with you," I tried to reassure her. "I just want the best possible program for us."

Usually, she wouldn't argue with me, but her grip tightened on her mug as she stared back at me, her gaze unwavering. "Put yourself in my shoes, Austin. You already left me to skate with her once before. What are people going to think when they see her on the ice with you?"

It honestly hadn't crossed my mind to be concerned about that, especially since it wasn't common knowledge that Grace had been my partner before Amy. Maybe she'd forgotten that, so I decided to remind her.

"Hardly anyone knows that you and I skated together before. Amy doesn't even know. I never told her."

My hope that Grace would find that reassuring proved to be unfounded. If anything, her concern deepened, her bottom lip trembling for a second before she pressed her lips tightly together.

"You skated with her for three years and you never talked about me?"

Well, when she phrased it that way, it didn't sound good.

"Neither of us talked about our former partners," I tried to explain. "You and I don't spend our time on the ice talking about Amy either."

I left out the part where I originally lied to Amy and told her my former partner had quit. That definitely wouldn't help. Eventually, I told Amy the truth about how I left my previous partner for her, but I never told her who that partner was.

Grace and I never skated competitively. We went into the test stream instead, and Grace remained there after I left, all the way up until she started training with me again. We'd been so young that there wasn't any public record of us skating together before I started competing with Amy, and we never mentioned it in interviews because of Grace's sensitivity over the perception that she hadn't been good enough.

I could see things from Grace's point of view, I really could, but it didn't change the fact that I still wanted to bring Amy on board.

"Even so, if she joins our team, people will think she wants to skate with you again," she argued, her face still lined with concern.

"No one will think that. It's four months until the Olympics. Nobody changes partners at a time like this."

"Or maybe they'll think you're dating her and that's why we hired her," she tried next. "If people found out that you and I aren't really seeing each other..."

Her other arguments, I tried to understand, but when it came to the ridiculous notion that Grace and I needed to pretend to be a couple in order to win, I didn't even let her finish.

"We can't control what people think. And I'm *not* dating her, so it's not an issue."

Way too much still needed to be settled between Amy and me before I could even think about a relationship with her, so telling Grace how much the idea appealed to me seemed premature at best and downright foolish at worst. I stuck to the facts instead.

"Look, you know how helpful she was to us already. Those things she fixed in our program really helped. On top of that, you saw the video of her other program, the one she created four years ago."

Grace tensed as soon as I mentioned the video. "That program was very obviously created for you and her. It's your style, not ours. If I try to skate like her..."

She trailed off, but I didn't need her to finish to understand that she was afraid of being compared to Amy, yet again.

"We're not going to skate that program," I reminded her. "Amy's going to work with us to create something just for us. I know her. She'll want to create something that highlights your strengths and makes you look as good as possible. Do you remember when she was on the ice with us, how she asked you how things felt and what you thought about things? Armand never did that."

Despite the truth in what I said, I could see my words weren't having the desired impact. Something else was still bothering her.

"I wanted to ask you about that. Why did she pretend to be someone else when she was interviewing you? What was the point of all of that?"

That was a damn good question, and one I still couldn't even fully answer for myself. I had some idea, but until we fully addressed the past, I wouldn't be able to fully understand.

"We have some things to talk through," I admitted. "But one thing you need to know about Amy is that she'll never let anything that's happening off the ice affect her work *on* the ice. She's the most dedicated dancer I've ever met. Even if she hates me, she'll design the best program she can for us."

Curiosity sparked in Grace's eyes, overtaking her concern for the first time since she sat down. "Why would she hate you?"

Getting into the details of the whole situation with Grace couldn't appeal to me less. The only person I wanted to talk about it with was Amy herself. "It's complicated, but the reason I want to work with her isn't. She's our best chance to get the program we need. I want to win, and I know you do too, so trust me, okay? If Amy designs our program, it will be the best one we've ever done."

She searched my face for a long moment, looking for something in my eyes, though I couldn't guess what. "And you promise this won't be a distraction?"

Could I promise that? Amy had certainly distracted me ever since she turned up again, but she also made me want to work harder and be better. In the long run, it would be worth it.

"I'm focused on the season, Grace: you and me and the Olympics. That's what this has all been for, right?"

Finally, a small smile graced her face. "Right. Okay. If you're sure, then I guess it's okay with me."

Relief filled me as I walked Grace back to the door and closed it behind her, resting my forehead on the cool wood for a moment after she'd gone. My mom was temporarily sidelined and Grace was on board. All that remained was Amy actually agreeing to do it.

Chapter Fourteen

~**Amelia**~

"Look straight into the camera and smile," the security guard at the skating club instructed as I posed for my new photo ID. Despite the pounding of my heart and the unsettled rolling of my stomach, I forced my mouth into an upward curve.

Although I spent several days at the rink during my profile interviews with Austin, arriving for my first day as a paid consultant felt completely different. The expectations on me were on a new and much higher level. The contract I signed stated I was a choreographer, officially there to design a new free dance for Austin and Grace that would be worthy of an Olympic medal.

Nobody knew for sure if I could actually do that, least of all myself, but if they didn't win that medal, it wouldn't be for lack of effort on my part.

Once I had checked in, I made my way into the changing room marked on the printed-out map I'd been given. A couple of women loitered on the benches inside and they looked over at me curiously when I entered.

Pasting the same smile from earlier back on my face, I greeted them as confidently as I could while still trying to sound friendly. "Hi there. Is this where the coaches get ready?"

"It is," one of the women replied. "Are you looking for someone?"

She must have assumed I was a skater rather than part of the coaching team. Not knowing how much had been shared about me prior to my arrival, I kept my response to the point.

"Sort of. My name's Mia and I'm looking for Brian Sills. He said I should meet him here."

"Oh, are you the new choreographer? The one Cynthia Black has been yelling about?" The woman's eyes sparkled with what looked like amusement.

I could only imagine what Austin's mother had to say about me being brought in. Austin must have filled her in on my real identity, and I couldn't imagine she would like me any more now than she ever had before.

"Probably. Exactly how mad is she?"

Both women laughed before the other one answered me. "You know her, then?"

I joined in their laughter, relieved to know they seemed to share my opinion of Mrs Black. The question also suggested that they didn't know about my history with her, for which I was grateful. "I've dealt with her before."

"Well, you're in luck. I haven't seen her yet today. I'm Andrea," the first woman introduced herself. "I coach some of the singles ladies, and Meghan works with some of our pairs."

"Really nice to meet you both," I said, placing my bag down on one of the benches. They were both older, probably in their forties, and I knew both of them by reputation. As usual, I had already done my research on the main coaches at the club. I liked to be prepared.

Brian walked in a couple of minutes later and Andrea and Meghan left, leaving Brian and me alone. We had spoken on the phone when I had returned his call, but this was our first time meeting properly in person. A former skater himself, now in his fifties, he had a reputation for being serious and disciplined on the ice. I anticipated our working relationship would remain strictly professional, so it threw me when he approached me with a friendly smile.

"Do I call you Mia or Amy?" he asked, raising a curious eyebrow at me. "Austin keeps referring to you as Amy, and I don't want to complicate things when I introduce you to people."

"I'm sorry for any confusion. My name's Amelia, and I used to go by Amy. Now, it's Mia, and that's what I'd preferred to be called."

"Mia it is, then. Now, to the business at hand. We're excited to have you here. I assume you saw the free dance at Skate America?"

"I did," I replied.

"And?"

He left the question there, completely open-ended, and for a moment, I wondered if I should try to be polite or skip the pleasantries and be direct.

Memories of Austin grinning at me whenever I spoke my mind flitted through my head. He'd always appreciated my brutal honesty, and I could only guess that was the reason he had wanted to bring me in. Best to start off that way then.

"It belongs on the junk heap. All of it."

Brian's eyes widened for just a second before he chuckled. "That seemed to be what the judges thought too. As I told you on the phone, Austin and Grace were meant to be competing at the Cup of China next week, but if we have no free dance, then it's probably better that we withdraw. It was their non-scoring event anyway. That makes their last Grand Prix event the NHK Trophy in Japan, in four weeks' time. That gives you four weeks to get them comfortable with an entirely new program. It's a tall order, Mia."

He wasn't kidding, but I already had the program half-created in my head, and I knew that Austin and Grace were willing to work hard at it. I'd already seen their work ethic while profiling Austin, and I couldn't imagine Austin had gotten any lazier since we trained together.

I really believed we could do it.

"Obviously, this is going to be our priority," Brian continued. "So, I'll work with you to give you as much ice time with them as you need. Let's sit down again after today's session to look at the schedule."

"That sounds great. Thank you." His faith in me made me wonder exactly what Austin had told him, but I appreciated it nonetheless.

Brian told me he preferred to stay off the ice as much as possible but that I could do whatever worked for me. I knew immediately that meant being on the ice. I needed to see everything up close, to hear their blades and see the small changes in their bodies as they performed the moves. I wanted to be able to demonstrate things when necessary and adjust their positioning.

It would mean touching them a lot. Touching *Austin* a lot. Hopefully, it wouldn't be as awkward as it sounded.

With all of that settled, I laced up my skates and headed out to the rink.

By the time I reached the ice, the skaters were already out doing their warm-up, and my eyes immediately found Austin. It was hard *not* to watch him. He stood out in every crowd, but especially on the ice.

Watching him move, a thrill of excitement shivered through my body at the idea of creating a dance especially for him and to see him performing the steps that I created, even if I wasn't the one doing them with him.

We hadn't spoken again since I called him just after I found out he shared the video, and we left things in an awkward place then. Therefore, his tentative smile didn't surprise me when I skated over to him and Grace as they finished their warm-up. However, if I acted professionally, I hoped he would follow suit and we could leave all of our personal issues in the past where they belonged.

IT FIGURES

"Hi, Grace," I said, speaking to her first, before turning to her partner. "Austin. I'm excited to be working with you both."

Grace didn't react in any way, her expression carefully blank, while Austin simply nodded in agreement.

I pressed on ahead despite their reactions. "You both know we don't have a lot of time to waste. I already have quite a few ideas but I want you to feel free to tell me if they're not working for you, or if you want to make any changes. This is collaborative, okay? At the end of the day, you're the ones who have to go out there and skate the program, so you need to feel comfortable with it."

Austin nodded again, a smile flashing across his face for the briefest moment. "We're in your hands, Amy."

A flush crept up my cheeks at the idea of Austin in my hands, but I forced it back down. *Professional relationship only.*

Grace said nothing, simply watching me with that same impassive expression. It seemed I would have my work cut out to win her over, but I fully intended to. The Olympics might be their fairy-tale ending, but it could be my new beginning. We all had a lot riding on this.

"In that case, let's get started."

~Austin~

It came as no surprise to me that Amy got straight down to business on the ice. I wouldn't have expected her to be any other way.

I could also tell from Grace's defensive posture when Amy first came over to us that she'd prepared herself not to like Amy. However, by the end of the session, her attitude had completely changed. Grace was buzzing. We both were.

The ideas that Amy had were exactly what we wanted to do for years, the kind of program we wanted to skate without even knowing it ourselves. Amy had already watched all of our old programs, picking out the ones that worked best for Grace, and used that as a foundation. It almost felt like she'd crawled inside our heads, like she could tell what would feel best for Grace and me.

It would have been impossible not to be impressed.

When the session ended, I waited until we were off the ice and Grace had already headed back towards the locker room before making my way over to where Amy stood, talking to Brian. Brian had completely let her take the lead today, just watching from the boards, so they seemed to be comparing notes. I probably shouldn't interrupt, but I needed to talk to her.

Now that I knew that she thought I had ended our partnership by choice, I needed to set the record straight.

Brian gave me a nod as I approached. "It looked good out there, Austin. How did that feel for you?"

Our training *should* have been forefront in my thoughts, so I played along, pretending that was why I came over in the first place. "It felt good. I'm excited to see what Amy creates for us."

Her cheeks tinted even though she didn't look at me, and I had to smile. She never could take a personal compliment. It seemed that hadn't changed.

"Can I talk to you, Amy?" I asked, eager to get her alone.

When she looked up at me, the confident woman from out on the ice had disappeared. In her place, the scared, hurt girl who'd argued with me at the rink the last time we were together stared back at me.

"I'll give you a minute," Brian said, excusing himself. "Amy... I mean Mia, sorry. I'll catch up with you in the locker room."

He walked away and I turned my full attention to Amy. "You're still having people call you Mia?"

"It's my name," she said before taking a deep breath and looking me in the eye. "What do you need, Austin?"

"I need to talk to you. In private. Away from the rink."

"I don't think we have anything to talk about outside the rink," she claimed.

"That's not true," I countered, just as firmly. "I've learned something that's important for you to know, but I don't want to tell you here. Just give me a bit of time. Please. I'm free all day tomorrow."

We usually only trained one day of the weekend when it wasn't a competition weekend, and that week, we had Saturday off.

Her eyes drifted up, as if reviewing the calendar in her head. "I have plans for lunch, but I could meet you later in the afternoon. For coffee or something."

I knew exactly what she was doing: trying to meet me in a public place where things couldn't get too personal. It wouldn't be my preference, but if it was that or nothing, I would take it. We simply needed to talk, I wouldn't stress about the venue.

"Okay. Since you're the one with plans, text me where and when to meet you."

She agreed, and I headed back to the locker room, feeling a little bit lighter than before. It wouldn't be an easy conversation, but after all these years, some of the unsaid things that had piled up between us were finally going to be said.

Hopefully, it wouldn't be too late.

~Amelia~

As I got dressed on Saturday morning, I could barely believe the day I had ahead of me. How did this become my life? First, I had lunch plans with Paul where he would also give me some photography tips, and afterwards, I would meet Austin for coffee.

I had no idea what Austin wanted to talk about, but if something was bothering him, it would be better to get it out in the open. Since we were going to work together, we needed to be able to trust each other.

In the spirit of clearing the air, I met with Samantha, the editor-in-chief at Urban Style, once I got back from the training session with Austin and Grace the day before. With my new job, the article I wrote might start to look biased, which was ironic since I'd kept my identity hidden to avoid that in the first place.

I confessed everything to Samantha: all about my past, how I used to skate with Austin, and how I hid my identity from him while doing the profile. She must have been shocked, but she covered it pretty well. The rather stern lecture she gave me about journalistic integrity came as no surprise.

However, when she finished giving me the talking-to I deserved, she leaned back in her chair and smiled. "My niece is going to be so jealous that you actually got to skate with him when she reads the article."

My mouth fell open before I could stop it. "You're still going to print it?"

I'd been fully prepared for her to tell me they were cutting it, and possibly ending my internship too.

"We're not dealing with life-or-death news here," she told me with a laugh. "It's only a conflict if we're not up front about it. Since Austin is fine with it, we'll just add a paragraph at the beginning explaining your relationship. It actually makes the story even more interesting since you know him so well."

By the time I left her office, I felt a million times better than when I walked in. I could have saved myself so much stress and worry if I'd just been up front with her from the beginning.

I would do my best to remember that in the future.

Paul met me by the waterfront just before noon, waving me over to where he stood with two large camera cases. The mid-October sun glistened off the lake and I let my eyes sweep over Paul as I approached. When I stopped to think about it, I could see his charm. Tall and lanky, with slightly curly blond hair and a neatly trimmed beard, he would make a lot of women look twice.

I'd never really thought of him that way before, but maybe I should. It didn't hurt to be open to things.

He gave me a quick hello kiss on the cheek and filled me in on his plans. "I don't want us to have to lug these cases too far, so I thought we could just grab some hot dogs for lunch, if that's okay."

Immediately, I felt silly for the path my thoughts had just taken. That didn't sound much like a date, so maybe I had read too much into his lunch invitation. Either way, I agreed to the hot dogs, and we picked up a couple from the nearby stand before spending the next two hours taking photos.

Paul brought three different cameras with a variety of different lenses, and he lost me pretty quickly when he started explaining all the technical equipment. However, he gave me a lot of really good basic tips as well, and my photos at the end of the two hours looked a lot better than the ones I took at the beginning.

Paul often stood behind me to help me line up a shot, leaning over my shoulder and placing his hands on mine. It felt a bit intimate, but it could have also just been part of his teaching method. I really wasn't sure. He certainly didn't try to make any other move.

We talked a little as we worked. He asked me a bit more about my skating, since he had seen me on the ice with Austin, and I gave vague answers. Although I told Samantha the whole truth about my past, I still didn't want everyone knowing about it.

When he explained his reason for asking, I felt bad about being so cagey. "I'm curious because my brother used to skate as well, and now he's a journalist."

Hearing about someone else who followed roughly the same career path I was considering definitely caught my interest. "That's really cool. Where does he work?"

"He covers a few different sports, including figure skating. He writes for a website and he also does work for one of the networks, doing backstage interviews and stuff at the events."

Before I could ask any follow-up questions, a family of ducks came waddling down the path behind us on their way to the lake, and Paul quickly pointed my camera in that direction, helping me get a bunch of adorable photos.

When we finished, he offered to give me a ride back to campus, but since I had plans to meet Austin, I politely declined. Paul gave me another kiss on the cheek and said he would see me in the office.

Even at the end of our time together, I still couldn't say for sure if it had been a date or not.

In any case, I had a bit of time to kill before heading to the coffee shop to meet Austin, so I went for a stroll along the waterfront. The longer I walked, the more nervous I got.

What did he want to talk about? Was he finally going to explain why he never got in touch with me all those months? Or why he moved on to Grace without any kind of explanation? Would he finally tell me why he kissed me that night, and why he ran away afterwards?

Did I really want to dredge *any* of that up again?

Austin and I were going to be working together. Maybe we could even be friends with time but we were never going to be on-ice partners again, so why rehash everything? Wouldn't it be better to start fresh and move on?

My mom certainly thought so, and I thought I had too, but Austin's insistence about meeting to talk made me waver in that conviction. Since I'd promised to meet him, it seemed like I didn't have much choice at that point. One way or another, I'd have to listen to whatever he wanted to tell me.

Chapter Fifteen

~**Austin**~

My throat tightened painfully as Amy came through the door of the coffee shop. Swallowing felt like sandpaper rubbing against my vocal cords. Even though I'd seen her a few times by that point, I still found it hard to believe that, after all this time, she was actually there in front of me. Part of me still thought it might be a dream; a long and sustained one, for sure, but a dream nonetheless. At any moment, I might wake up and find her gone again, and that thought frightened me most of all.

So, although the things I needed to say to her weren't going to be easy, I still felt grateful for the chance to finally say them.

"Do you want a drink?" I asked when she arrived at the table, taking a sip from my own tea to wet my lips and throat, both dry with nerves. "I can grab something for you."

She removed her coat and slung it across the back of her chair before taking a seat. In a sweater and jeans, the casualness of her clothes contrasted with the guarded tightness of her body, her expression carefully blank as she lowered herself into the chair. Her glasses were starting to seem familiar, and over the scent of coffee and baking that filled the air, I caught a whiff of her perfume too, the new scent she wore that would always make me think of Mia, even though I now knew they were one and the same.

"I'm okay. What did you want to talk to me about?"

Straight to the point, just like she'd always been on the ice. That confidence used to inspire me, and I used to hope it would bleed over into her personality off the ice too. I always wanted everyone else to see the amazing, driven girl I got to see on a daily basis.

Knowing she would appreciate it, I decided to be just as blunt with her in return, diving straight in.

"My mom lied to me after your accident. She told me that you decided to quit skating. I thought you weren't coming back, Amy. That's why I left to train with Grace. That's the *only* reason I moved on."

Amy's brows tightened, forming two deep vertical lines above her nose, while her eyes searched mine. I forced myself to meet her gaze as calmly as I could, keeping my expression as open as possible. I could see she didn't know whether or not to believe me, and that uncertainty hurt. She used to trust me. Could we ever get back there again?

"Why didn't you tell me that right away, when you figured out who I was?" she finally asked.

"I didn't know it then. I only found out the other day. Once my mom realized we were going to be working together again, she finally told me. I guess she decided it would be better for her to tell me before you got a chance to. Thinking of herself, as usual."

Amy's eyes moved away from me, confusion written across her face. "Even if that were true..." she started to say, and I quickly interrupted.

"It *is* true. I wouldn't lie to you."

Her grimace served as a reminder that I *had* lied to her, not that long ago, about not sharing the video with anyone. I really hadn't done myself any favours with her by doing that, but if I hadn't done it, we wouldn't be working together or even sitting there together. In the end, I couldn't fully regret that decision.

"I wouldn't lie to you about this," I amended.

"But you had to know I would never quit." Her eyes darted back to me, a frisson of electricity passing through me as our stares collided. "No matter what, that's the one thing you should have known."

The quiet words pierced my heart as much as if she had shouted them, and suddenly, I found myself blinking back tears. Was she right? *Should* I have known it was a lie? Should I have trusted in her more than that? Confused and hurt by her silence, I trusted my mom, a person I should have been able to trust more than anyone.

Could I have done it differently?

"Why didn't you call me?" I asked, moving on to the one thing I wanted to know most of all. "All those months, I didn't know where you were, where you'd gone. I would have been there for you. I would have helped you, done physio with you, trained with you, whatever you needed. Why did you hide from me?"

The tears in my eyes slipped down my cheeks as all the years of bottled-up hurt and rejection opened at once. I quickly brushed the tears away, aware that we were still in public and not wanting to make a scene.

The emotion didn't just belong to me, though. Amy's equally red eyes looked back at me from behind her glasses.

"You never even came to see me," she whispered, speaking so quietly that I had to lean forward to hear her. "I was in the hospital for a week, and you never came."

What on earth was she talking about? Of course I went, and the only reason I didn't go back was because her mom told me I wasn't welcome. Amy didn't want to see me. Surely, she had to remember that.

"I tried," I reminded her, the lump in my throat getting bigger by the second, making it harder to breathe. "I came as soon as I heard but your mom told me to go. I waited with my phone in my hand, every day, hoping you would call, hoping you would say you wanted to see me and that you didn't hate me."

Tears dropped from her eyes, and she pulled her glasses off, rubbing at the wetness on her face with the sleeves of her sweater. "Of course I didn't hate you. Nobody ever said that you came."

Why wouldn't her parents have told her? They both saw me, spoke to me. Her mom did more than speak; she hurled all the blame and recriminating words that had been swirling around in my head straight into my face.

It didn't make any sense that they lied, but the look in Amy's eyes left no doubt that her words were true. She honestly thought I never even tried to come and see her.

How could she think that?

How could I think that she would really quit without telling me? How had we gotten to the point where we disregarded everything we knew about each other? Did that kiss really throw us off that much?

"Why didn't you text me back?" I asked next. If she didn't hate me after all, why did she ignore all my messages? "I wrote to you all the time. Why didn't you ever write back?"

Fresh tears formed in her eyes. "You texted me?"

"Of course I did. Every day."

She shook her head, denying it, or maybe just indicating that she didn't want it to be true. "I lost my phone in the accident. It was destroyed and I didn't have your number. My mom said she gave you my new one, so I waited. I waited every day for you to call me. You never texted me on that number."

A gaping emptiness opened inside me as all the pieces began to fall into place.

She never got my messages. I thought she was ignoring me, too angry with me to even talk to me, when in reality she had never seen them at all. Meanwhile, she thought I was ignoring *her* instead, but no one ever told me she had a new number.

I thought I'd experienced all the pain I ever could from losing her, but somehow, this felt even worse. Knowing that she didn't hate me at all, that she hadn't been trying to punish me, was worse than thinking she had.

I didn't need to explain any of those thoughts to Amy. In her face, I could see every realization I had, every emotion I felt, reflected right back at me.

I kept moving the conversation forward instead.

"Where did you go? I went to your house after you were discharged to see you but no one was there. When I went back a few days later, your dad only told me that you went away to recover."

"My mom and I went to St John's to stay with my aunt and work on my physio. I worked so hard, Austin. All I wanted was to get back to you, to our training..."

She broke off as a sob escaped her lips, choking off her words, and her hands covered her face, hiding the worst of her anguish from me. Both of us felt it at the same time, finally comprehending the awful truth.

She didn't want to stop skating with me and I didn't want to stop skating with her.

I should have trusted that more, and she should have trusted it too.

We had been in such a weird place after our kiss, and I thought...

I thought...

In the end, it didn't matter what I thought. What I thought was wrong, and I screwed up. I lost my partner and the girl I cared for more than anything and I hurt her terribly in the process. I could see that as plain as day on her face and hear it in the sniffles she made as she reached for a napkin from the table to dry her eyes.

At least I was still skating. I still had that vital part of myself intact. What would it have been like for Amy, losing not only our partnership but the sport she loved so passionately too? I really couldn't even imagine.

Would there ever be a way for me to make it up to her? Could we ever make it right?

Before I could say anything else, a group of girls approached our table, and my heart sank as I realized what was happening. They recognized me. Sitting there with tears still in my eyes, talking to fans was not my priority, but there was nowhere to hide.

I ducked my head to wipe my face dry and tried to look calm and collected as I looked back up.

"Excuse me, are you Austin Black?" one of them asked, holding onto her phone while her friends crowded in beside me.

Amy hadn't seen them approaching, so she looked up in surprise when the girl spoke, quickly shoving her glasses back on to hide her puffy face as the situation became clear to her.

"Yeah," I replied, trying to smile as if my heart weren't splintered into a million pieces. "Are you guys skating fans?"

"Yes!" they squealed. "You and Grace are so good."

I couldn't look at Amy to see her reaction. I knew if I did, I would start crying again.

"Thanks," I managed to say.

"Could we get a picture?" the one with the phone asked. I expected the request, but it still made me wince. I could only imagine what my face looked like and I didn't think I could smile if my life depended on it.

But to my great surprise, Amy reached out her hand for the phone. "Here, let me take it. You guys all get in."

The girls grinned at her happily and they all crowded around me while Amy lined up the shot. Just before she took the picture, she stuck her tongue out at me, and I laughed in surprise, completely taken off guard. Obviously, that had been her plan, and she snapped the photo as I smiled.

"There you go," she said, handing the phone back to its owner. They thanked her and me before leaving us alone. Unfortunately, the interaction attracted other attention, and several more people had started looking our way.

"I think we should go," I said, though I still had so many more things I wanted to say to her.

"Probably," she agreed, grabbing her coat and putting it on. "I'm going to walk back to campus. You can walk with me if you want to."

I gratefully agreed and we set out together into the rapidly darkening October afternoon.

~Amelia~

The brisk air quickly found the traces of tears still on my cheeks, sending a chill through me. I wiped my face with my sleeves once more while Austin fell into step beside me as we headed up Yonge Street, away from the lake. I shoved my hands in my pockets and he did the same, walking close enough to me to talk but far enough that I could feel the space between our bodies, a space that was bigger than it used to be when we were young, but a lot smaller than it felt over the past few weeks.

I could hardly wrap my head around everything he told me and how my parents lied to me. They never told me that he had tried to see me in the hospital. Why didn't he know about my new phone number? My mom told me she gave it to him; did she lie about that too? She knew how much it devastated me that he never got in touch, so I couldn't understand why she would have kept it from me.

On the other hand, I knew in my heart that Austin wasn't lying about any of it. The pain in his eyes was too real, too familiar.

He honestly believed that I chose not to see him and chose to stop skating with him. He believed it for years, the same way I believed he left me behind without a second thought.

How on earth did we get to this point?

How could we come back from it?

"Will you tell me about the accident?" he asked, his voice low and quiet as he walked beside me. "No one ever told me the details and I always wanted to know."

Tears welled up in my eyes again, but I forced them away with a furious blink, looking down at the sidewalk in front of me. "I don't remember the accident. One minute, I was walking down the street, and the next, I woke up in the hospital. Apparently, a car jumped the curb and hit me, but I don't remember any of that. I don't remember feeling any pain."

His shuddering breath clenched around my heart, and I couldn't look up at him, not if I wanted to keep from crying again.

"They had to do surgery on my leg, but my arm only needed to be set. I stayed in the hospital for a week. After that, we drove to St John's."

"You drove?"

The question seemed so unimportant in the grand scheme of things, it almost made me laugh. I had to remember that since he didn't know anything, it probably all felt important to him. I could understand that. If our situations were reversed, I would have wanted to know every detail too.

"I couldn't really fly with my casts, so yeah. My parents set me up in the back of our van, propped up with pillows. We drove to Nova Scotia and took the ferry from there."

"How long did that take?"

Austin sounded completely bewildered, and I found myself smiling in spite of everything. "Two days in total. It felt a lot longer though."

There had been nothing for me to do in the van other than try to read one-handed, which got old very fast. I lay there, feeling every bump in the road reverberating through my sore, achy body, listening to the hum of the van's motor, and trying to come up with new programs in my head, new things that Austin and I could try once we got back on the ice.

"And then?" he prompted, still wanting to know more.

"When we arrived, I started a rehab program with my aunt. It took just over two months to get the casts off and another four months before the doctor cleared me to go back on the ice."

I chanced a glance up at him, and I could almost see him doing the calculations in his head, trying to figure out at what point I found out that he decided to skate with Grace.

"Why didn't you let Karen know you were coming back?" he asked, his voice gone quiet again.

There was no accusation in the question, just a deep sadness that I recognized very well. The same feeling had taken up residence deep inside me as the full scope of our lost possibilities became clear.

"I thought we did. My mom said we did. However, she never told me that you came to the hospital, so maybe she lied about keeping Karen updated too."

"And my mom lied to me." His face clouded over with anger for a moment. "I really can't believe all this, Amy. If I had thought for one second that you were coming back..."

"I know." I cut him off, unwilling to go down that road. It was far too late for 'what ifs'. They wouldn't change anything, wouldn't accomplish anything other than wasting our time and energy. "I don't blame you, Austin. You did what was best for you, and obviously it's worked out for you and Grace."

"I would rather be skating with you."

The simple, earnest sincerity in his statement nearly took my breath away, leaving me with no choice but to believe him.

And yet, we both knew it was too late. We couldn't change what happened, and we couldn't change the future either. A matter of months stood between him and an Olympic medal. He couldn't stop skating with Grace to skate with me, and I didn't want him to. I didn't want him to lose everything he'd worked so hard for.

"If you're skating my program, it'll almost be like I'm out there with you," I offered instead, feeling a little ridiculous for trying to comfort him about the fact that he would be going to the Olympics and I wouldn't.

"I want you to be there," he said, turning to look at me with a plea in his eyes. "At the Games, I mean. I want you to come with us."

That wouldn't be impossible. Choreographers sometimes attended competitions too. If he really wanted me there, and if I wanted to go, we might be able to make it happen.

"We'll see," I replied, not wanting to commit to anything right away after all the emotional upheaval of the day. "I still have school and other things going on."

He asked me about school and I finally got to open up to him and answer some of the questions he tried to ask me when he still thought of me only as Mia. I told him how I'd started writing once it became clear I wouldn't be going back to training full-time. I started reporting on local sports news for one of the St John's papers and from there, I decided to study journalism at university. I told him about the internship at the magazine and we talked a little about the article I'd written about him.

I took the opportunity to apologize once again for lying to him. "I thought you wanted nothing to do with me," I explained as gently as I could. "I didn't think you would want to see me again."

He shook his head, pain still in his eyes. "That was never how I felt, Amy, and it never will be."

Something shifted in his expression, his teeth grazing over his lower lip as he carefully considered his next words.

"I know it was four years ago and everything has changed since then, but we never got to talk about what happened that night when I dropped you off."

Our kiss, he meant. The thought of it sent a shiver down my spine, especially when his tongue ran over his lips, waiting for my response.

We probably should talk about it, but after all the revelations of the afternoon, I didn't think I could handle another emotional conversation. I needed a bit of time to recover first.

Luckily for me, we had arrived on campus, so I had an excuse.

"This is my building," I told him, pointing at the dorm across the street. "I need to get back in and have supper before the cafeteria closes."

His eyes scanned the dorm curiously, a dozen new questions swimming in his gaze, but we'd never get through everything we both wanted to know in one night.

He must have reached the same conclusion, because he exhaled, looking back over at me with resignation. "Alright. I'll see you at the rink tomorrow, right?"

"I'll be there. Do you need directions to the subway or anything? Where are you going now?"

His lips curled into a sheepish smile. "My car's back at the waterfront. I'll walk back down."

My eyes widened in dismay. I wouldn't have made him walk all the way to campus with me if I knew it was completely out of his way.

"It's okay," he assured me, reading my feelings in my face as easily as he used to. "I wanted the chance to talk to you. And Amy, there's still one more thing I need to say."

His expression turned completely serious again, and I tried to brace myself for whatever it might be. After everything he already revealed to me, I couldn't begin to guess what else was left to be said.

He took a deep breath, as if steeling himself, and when he spoke again, his voice came out soft but firm. "I'm so sorry I didn't give you a ride that day."

The tears I thought I had vanquished reappeared in an instant as I heard the pain infusing each word. "It's not your fault, Austin. It never was. You couldn't have known."

He looked away from me, his lower lip trembling, and sympathy, strong and deep, rushed through me. Had he really been blaming himself all this time? That idea broke my heart. Even at my lowest moments, I never wanted him to feel that.

Without planning to, I surprised the both of us by reaching my hand up to his face and turning it back towards me. His eyes remained down, his lashes hiding whatever emotion lurked in them. "I mean it," I told him firmly. "I never blamed you. It was just a random, stupid thing that happened, and it had absolutely nothing to do with you."

"But if I..." he started.

"No." I cut him off firmly, as convinced of what I was about to say as I had ever been of anything in my life. "We can't know what would have happened. What if I had left a minute earlier or a minute later? What if I called a cab or took the bus? What if that driver went down a different street or got stopped at a red light? There are a million what ifs, Austin, and you're just one of them. You didn't do this. It's not your fault."

His eyes finally met mine, tears hovering in their corners. I couldn't tell if my words convinced him, but I hoped he heard me anyway and that he would think about it.

"I'm still sorry anyway," he whispered.

"Me too."

There was nothing else to say.

He nodded as a tear escaped and rolled down his cheek. "Okay. Good night, Amy. Thank you for talking to me, and I guess I'll see you on the ice tomorrow."

"See you tomorrow," I agreed, giving him one final tearful smile before he turned and walked away.

Chapter Sixteen

~Austin~

The city around me barely registered in my subconscious as I walked back to my car. Despite the rumble of the subway beneath my feet, the honking of cars and chattering of tourists around me, my thoughts were far away, going over everything Amy told me. There was a lot to process, but one thing stood out above all the others.

Amy didn't blame me for the accident.

It never occurred to me she wouldn't. I'd felt it deep in my bones when it happened and her mom had confirmed it at the hospital: the whole thing was my fault. I'd never doubted it, so Amy's calm certainty that I bore no more responsibility than she did felt like someone had shoved me onto the ice with skates that were too sharp. From the outside, everything looked the same, but my internal balance had been completely thrown off.

Maybe if I hadn't felt so guilty, if I hadn't been so sure that she must have blamed me too, I would have been more suspicious when my mom announced Amy's retirement. Maybe I should have been suspicious when she set me up to skate with Grace again in the first place.

Maybe I had let my remorse blind me to the truth, which was that Amy would have never given up on us.

Not *on* the ice, anyway.

There were so many 'what ifs', and nothing I could do about any of them. The cold, hard truth was that I couldn't change the past, and Amy had rightly pointed out that regrets were useless. We could only look forward.

So, what did that future look like?

We'd talked about the accident, but we still needed to talk about our kiss and everything that took place in the days leading up to the accident. Although it might be too late for any kind of relationship between us, I owed her an explanation for what happened that night, even if the explanation seemed weaker than ever with the passing of the years.

However, if I wanted to be honest with myself, I hoped it *wasn't* too late for something between us. Even though she looked different, I still found her as attractive as I always had. She must have changed over the past four years, and I had too, but when we were together, it felt the same.

It felt like there was nowhere else I'd rather be.

~Amelia~

With everything Austin and I talked about still fresh in my mind that evening, I decided to head back to my dorm room alone while my friends went to a movie after dinner. I needed answers. I needed to talk to my parents and find out exactly what happened and why they lied to me. If I truly wanted to put the past to rest, once and for all, I needed to know everything.

It made sense to start with my dad. He might not know as much about what happened during my recovery, but he'd always been more objective about the accident than my mom. At the very least, he should be able to tell me if he saw Austin at the hospital.

He answered on the second ring. "Hi, Mia."

My new name never sounded natural coming from his mouth. He tried his best to use it, but because I didn't see him or talk to him anywhere near as much as I did with my mom, it never sounded quite right.

"Hi, Dad. How are you? How's everyone there?"

My dad remarried the previous year. His new wife had two young kids, my step-siblings, but I had only met them once, at the wedding. He loved me, I never doubted that, but he had a whole new life I didn't really fit into. He probably felt the same way about me.

"We're good. How's life in TO?"

He always insisted on using a nickname for Toronto, as if it somehow made it more exciting rather than the place I chose to go to university to avoid the memories associated with Ottawa.

"It's been pretty interesting lately," I told him, getting to the point of my call. "I got in touch with Austin recently."

The pause on the other end of the line felt more like surprise than caution. My mom had been worried when I told her, probably because she worried that if Austin and I had a proper conversation, he would reveal her lies, exactly as he ended up doing.

From my dad, though, the silence felt more simple. He just hadn't seen it coming.

"Really? How did that go?"

"It's complicated," I admitted. "But he told me something that I want to ask you about. He said that he came to visit me in the hospital after my accident, but Mom sent him away. Do you know anything about that?"

The pause that time lasted longer, making me certain that he *did* know something. "Have you talked to your mom about it?"

I answered honestly "Not yet. I wanted to talk to you first. She gets a little defensive every time Austin is mentioned."

My dad exhaled, his breath unsteady. "This is probably why. She probably feels guilty."

Even though I didn't think Austin lied to me, my heart still sank with the confirmation. "She really did turn him away?"

"You know what your mom was like," he reminded me. "Keeping you safe was the most important thing in the world to her, and the accident nearly broke her. When Austin showed up to see you, your mom was in a really bad place and she was pretty hard on him."

"What did she say?"

The image of Austin's face with tears in his eyes as he blamed himself for what happened, swam in front of me. Did my mom have something to do with him feeling that way?

"I don't remember the exact words, but she told him not to come back until you asked for him. When she decided to move you to Newfoundland, Austin wasn't her top priority. I don't know if she ever got in touch with him."

"But I *did* ask for him," I pointed out. "I asked you both if I could talk to him."

My dad sighed again. "I know, but she thought you needed to focus on your recovery. She convinced me to let her do things her way because she knew what was best for you. After you two were gone... well, you'll have to talk to her about that part since she stopped talking to me then too."

Even four years on, I could hear the pain in my dad's voice, and another piece of the wider picture came into view. Our move to Newfoundland had been the catalyst for my parent's divorce. I understood that, but I had always attributed it to the physical distance. I never really considered that my mom's need to control my recovery played a part as well.

"If you talk to him again, would you tell him I'm sorry?" my dad asked. "I should have fought harder for him to get to see you. I'm sure it drove him crazy not to."

Once again, my eyes burned with tears. I thought I had cried myself out about the accident years ago, but learning all these new things I didn't know felt like ripping a scab off and letting the pain bleed out all over again.

"I'll tell him," I promised. "I'm actually going to be seeing a lot of him given that I'm working with him and his new partner on one of their programs."

"Really? Mia, that's amazing. You would be so good at that."

"Thanks, Dad. I better go for now. But I'll try to call again soon."

"Okay. I love you, honey. Sheryl says hi."

After I hung up, I stared at the phone in my hand, trying to decide if I should wait until the next day to talk to my mom. I already felt wrung out, but I would see Austin at the rink the next day, and I wanted to get everything clear in my head before I saw him again.

I wanted to know the full truth.

My mom *had* been very protective of me, as my dad said, but she'd gotten better about it. Without the spotlight of the skating world shining on me, she stopped thinking the whole world was out to take advantage of me, and she even let me go to Toronto for university by myself. I could almost forget just how overprotective she used to be.

But as I thought back to the time of the accident, it seemed plausible that she would have thought that keeping me in isolation would be the right thing to do, without ever stopping to consider how that would affect Austin. Had she really done it all on purpose?

My hands shaking, I placed the call.

It took my mom longer to answer. Just before her voicemail picked up, she did, the sound of rustling nearly drowning out her greeting. "Mia? What's going on? Is something wrong?"

"I'm okay, but I need to talk to you about Austin."

Just like every other time I mentioned his name to her recently, a long, drawn-out pause followed my statement. "What about him?"

"We talked about the accident and what happened afterwards. Is there anything you forgot to tell me about that week in the hospital?"

I hadn't meant it to sound quite so sarcastic, but I couldn't stop the bitterness from creeping into my voice as I remembered the tears in Austin's eyes and the many, many tears I'd shed over the years.

She didn't even pretend not to know what I meant, and my heart sank further with every quiet, apologetic word out of her mouth. "I'm sorry I never told you he came. I was just trying to protect you. At the time, I thought it was the right call."

My bitterness grew stronger as the weight of those wasted years pressed down on me. "I might be able to understand why you felt that way on that day, even though I don't agree, but what about all the years since then? You knew how much it hurt me that he never tried to reach me. The whole time, you knew he *did* try, and you never told me!"

"It was his fault that you got hurt in the first place, and then he…"

"Don't say that!" I cut her off in disbelief. "I never blamed him. You knew that too, but you let him think I did. He blamed himself for four years. He felt terrible about it because he thought I hated him the whole time. He thought I *hated* him, Mom."

All the pent-up emotion came pouring out of me like a tap fully opened as I finally let myself feel the full injustice of it.

"I lost my partner and my friend and my career, all because you couldn't accept that it was just an accident?"

"He still left you…" she tried to say, her own sobs choking her just as mine were strangling me.

"He didn't mean to. His mom lied to him and told him I wasn't coming back, and he believed her because he never heard a thing from me. And that was all because of you. Did you ever even give him my new number, or did you lie about that too?"

"I... well, I gave it to Karen to give to him." From the tremble in her voice, I could tell she was crying too, but at that point, her hurt feelings mattered to me a lot less than Austin's did.

"Did you give it to Mrs Black, like you told me you did?"

"No." The quiet admission landed on my heart with another cracking thud. "I couldn't bring myself to speak to that evil woman, knowing she was probably happy you were injured and out of her way."

That might have been true, but couldn't she have put her pride aside for my sake? It wasn't a good enough reason for Austin to spend all that time thinking I didn't want to talk to him. I didn't know why Karen hadn't passed it on, but it didn't matter as much to me as knowing the woman I trusted had let me down at one of the most vulnerable times in my life, and lied to me about it ever since.

"She might be evil, but her betrayal hurts a lot less than yours. You did this, Mom. You drove me and Austin apart, and ruined my career. All this time, you blamed him, but it was you."

"Amy, please..."

In her despair, she forgot to use my new name, and my heart hardened even further. All the pain, all the loss, all the hurt of the past four years rolled together, and I couldn't listen to another word. I hung up the phone and turned it off so that even if she tried to call back, I wouldn't know. Maybe she deserved to know how Austin felt when she cut him off, at least for a little while.

Everything I thought I knew over the past four years had been a lie, everything I'd built my new life on turned out to be false. The unexpected revelations shifted my foundations almost as much as that day waking up in the hospital bed did, and though I didn't know yet exactly what my future held, I did know one thing for sure: things were never going to be the same.

The Story Continues

Read the conclusion of Amy and Austin's story in the second book of the duet, *Figuring It Out*

Keep in Touch

For more about my other books and to keep up-to-date with new releases, find all the links here:
https://linktr.ee/melodytyden

www.ingramcontent.com/pod-product-compliance
Lightning Source LLC
Chambersburg PA
CBHW072049110526
44590CB00018B/3096